C000319669

THE EDINBURGH GUIDE

DAVID PERROTT

Robert Nicholson Publications

A Nicholson Guide
First published in 1988
© Robert Nicholson Publications 1988

Central Edinburgh map © John Bartholomew & Son
based upon the Ordnance Survey with the sanction of
the Controller of Her Majesty's Stationery Office.
Crown copyright reserved.

All other maps and plans
© Robert Nicholson Publications

Maps and plans by **Perrott Cartographics**

Illustrations by **Eileen Knight**

Cover photograph by Paul Tompkins. Photographic
section transparencies from Scottish Tourist Board,
Wade Cooper Associates and Ann MacDougall

Robert Nicholson Publications
16 Golden Square
London W1R 4BN

Great care has been taken throughout this book to be
accurate, but the publishers cannot accept
responsibility for any errors which appear or their
consequences.

Typeset by The Word Factory, Rossendale, Lancs
Printed by Scotprint Ltd, Musselburgh

ISBN 0 94857616 2

88/1/120

Introduction

It is often said that Edinburgh is one of Europe's most beautiful and historic capitals, worthy of comparison with Athens and Rome. Beneath the dark volcanic outcrop of Castle Rock the great pageant of Scottish history has been enacted, and nowhere can the atmosphere of those turbulent times be captured more than in the rugged buildings and tangled courtyards of the Old Town. Yet just five minutes walk away is the polished Georgian elegance of the 18thC New Town, one of the finest examples of town planning to be seen anywhere.

Such a wealth of interest, tightly packed into the central square mile, makes Edinburgh an immensely rewarding place to visit, especially during the world-famous Festival. With all the information you need – on the sights, eating, drinking, shopping, the arts, the Festival, fishing and golf, day trips and vital tourist information – this guide will enable the visitor to make the most of everything Edinburgh has to offer.

The map references which appear
on the top right hand side of
entries refer to the central area
street map, pages 156-157.

Contents

A Glimpse of Scottish History

When Emperor Hadrian built his defensive wall from the Solway to the Tyne in AD **121**, it marked the northernmost stronghold of the Roman Empire. Further forays northwards were curtailed in the face of effective warfare waged by the Caledonians. The Roman fort at Cramond, and the Antonine Wall from the Forth to the Clyde were abandoned. Scotland was never a part of the Roman Empire, and was inhabited by four tribes: the Picts (of Celtic origin), who occupied the area north of the Forth; the Scots, Irish Celts who occupied Dalriada, what we now call Argyll; the Britons, another Celtic race living in what we now know as Strathclyde; and the Angles, Teutonic Anglo-Saxons who held the country south of the Forth. From the 5th to 7thC Christianity spread and the monastery of Candida Casa was founded by St Ninian in AD **398** at Whithorn, on the northern shore of the Solway Firth. His work was continued by such notables as St Columba, who established his base on Iona; St Moluag, who founded a religious settlement on Lismore, and St Maelrubba, who landed at Applecross. By the end of the 7thC Alban, as Scotland was then known, was almost completely converted to Christianity.

However, the four tribes were still not united, and proved unable to resist the Norse invasions of the northern and western islands, and the west coast. In AD **844** Kenneth MacAlpin, King of the Scots of Dalriada, was the one man strong enough to assert his claim over both kingdoms. He overcame the Picts (who were weakened by the aggression of the Norsemen) to be crowned King of Alban at Scone. The land north of the Forth was now united, but it was not until **1018**, when his descendant Malcolm II defeated the Angles at the Battle of Carham, that the territory south of the River Tweed came under his rule. In the same year, following the death of the King, Strathclyde was conquered by Malcolm, who then became the first King of Scotland. He died in **1034**, and was succeeded by Duncan I, followed by the powerful politician Macbeth and in **1058** by Malcolm III (Canmore). Malcolm's English upbringing and English wife, Margaret, heralded the beginning of English and Norman involvement in Scottish affairs. Margaret died on Castle Rock and the small Norman chapel, Edinburgh's oldest ecclesiastical building, was built in her memory.

Malcolm moved his court south into Edinburgh, and began a series of raids across the border, which provoked William the Conqueror to invade Scotland in **1072**; Malcolm was forced to pay homage to him at Abernethy. In **1093** Malcolm was killed and there followed a succession of weak kings and a period of turmoil until his sixth son, David, came to the throne in **1124**. A well-educated and accomplished man, David succeeded in building many churches including Holyrood Abbey, completed Scotland's Romanisation begun by his mother Margaret and firmly established the feudal system, giving large areas of land to the great Anglo-Norman families. Although David consolidated the kingdom, the extreme west, and the islands, were still allied to Norway.

David was succeeded by Malcolm IV who, in turn, was followed by his brother William I, The Lion. William concluded a formal treaty with France in **1165** (known in perpetuity as the 'Auld Alliance') and unsuccessfully invaded Northumberland during the reign of Henry II. Defeated at Alnwick, he was made to sign the humiliating Treaty of Falaise at Falaise Castle in Normandy, putting the whole of Scotland under English feudal submission. This was, however, renounced in **1189** and there then followed a century of relative peace between the two countries.

In **1263** King Haco of Norway was defeated at Largs, thus ending the Norse invasion – three years later the Western Isles were ceded to Alexander III, King of Scotland. In **1286** Alexander fell from his horse and was killed. The only heir to the throne was his grandchild, Margaret, daughter of the King of Norway. Edward I of England proposed that Margaret should marry his son, and a treaty to this effect was signed in **1290**. It was clear what Edward, a ruthless and ambitious king, had in mind, but Margaret died in Orkney without an heir. Edward chose John Balliol as the successor, a weak nonentity, who was duly crowned at Scone in **1292**, and told that he should continue to subjugate Scotland to England. Even Balliol, known as the 'Toom Tabard' or 'Empty Coat', was not prepared to accept this. He revived the 'Auld Alliance' with France and prepared to attack northern England. Edward was well prepared and moved swiftly to take all of southern Scotland, garrisoning the castles as he went. He then returned to London, appointing the Earl of Surrey as Governor and taking the ancient crowning Stone of Scone with him. He considered his domination of Scotland complete.

William Wallace led the first Scottish rebellion, defeating the English under the Earl of Surrey at Stirling Bridge in **1297**, but was defeated by Edward at Falkirk the following year. He was finally executed in **1305**. Edward then attempted the union of the two countries, but these plans were interrupted by Robert Bruce, grandson of Bruce (a rival of John Balliol), who claimed the throne and was crowned King of Scotland at Scone in **1306**, only to be overpowered that same year by Edward's army led by the Earl of Pembroke at Methven Wood. When Edward I died in **1307** his son, Edward II, did not maintain English dominance over Scotland, and Bruce captured all the castles until only Stirling held out. It was here, at the Battle of Bannockburn in **1314**, that Bruce finally defeated the English and restored independence to Scotland. Bruce, the Patriot King, died in **1329** in Cardross, on the Clyde, and was succeeded by his son, David II. War with the English broke out again. David died in **1371** and the Crown passed to the House of Stewart through the marriage of Robert Bruce's daughter, Marjory, to Walter Stewart of Scotland, a dynasty that was to last until 1603. Robert II became the first Stewart king, but the omens for his success were mixed. The Scottish nation was financially crippled by the ransom extracted by the English after King David II's defeat at Neville's Cross in **1346**. On the other hand, the English were now totally involved in the Hundred Years War with France, to whom Scotland was closely allied, and had little incentive to take on the Scots as well.

Robert III's (1390–1406) command was usurped by the Barons, of whom the Douglases were the most powerful, and control passed into their hands. James I (1406–1437) attempted to restore order, and made many enemies for his trouble. He defeated Donald, Lord of the Isles, in **1411**, thus annexing the western extremities of the land, and in that same year founded the first Scottish University at St Andrews. He was later murdered by Sir Robert Graham, who was eager to put the Earl of Atholl on the throne. James II (1437–1460) finally broke the power of the troublesome Black Douglas family. He sided with Henry VI in the Wars of the Roses, but was unfortunately killed by an exploding cannon while besieging Roxburgh Castle, Kelso. James III (1460–1488) married Margaret, daughter of Christian I of Denmark, receiving Orkney and Shetland as a dowry. The kingdom was now more or less complete with

Edinburgh its undisputed capital.

James IV's reign (1488–1513) was a period of relative peace, order and prosperity, during which time he married Margaret Tudor, daughter of Henry VII of England (an event which led ultimately to the Union of the Crowns in 1603). In **1513** James invaded England as he was bound by the Auld Alliance to support France when invaded by Henry VIII in that year. James was defeated, and killed, at Flodden Field.

The unruly chiefs of the Western Highlands and Islands were quelled by James V (1513–1542), who was himself killed by the English at the Battle of Solway Moss. His daughter, Mary, became Queen when only one week old in **1542**. Henry VIII of England proposed she should marry his Protestant son Edward. The Scots refused, and were disastrously defeated at the Battle of Pinkie Cleugh in **1547**. Scotland, as in the past, turned to France for help, and Mary married the Dauphin. 'France and Scotland', the French king declared, 'are now one country.'

Meanwhile the Reformation of the Churches was taking shape, the greatest watershed in the history of Scotland. John Knox was the most inflential agent of the Reformation and managed to establish a democratic Presbyterian Kirk in Scotland and a Scottish system of education. The year **1560** was a momentous one for Scotland. The Queen Mother (Mary of Guise–Lorraine) died; the Treaty of Edinburgh provided for the withdrawal of all English and French troops from Scottish soil; the Auld Alliance was dead; John Knox drew up his Confession of Faith and the Scottish Parliament decreed that henceforth Scotland would be a Protestant country. A year later, upon the death of the Dauphin, Mary Queen of Scots returned from France and lived at the Palace of Holyroodhouse for six years following her marriage there in **1564** to Henry Lord Darnley. It was not a happy relationship – Darnley would often leave the Palace of an evening to enjoy the dubious pleasures of the Royal Mile, and Mary denied him any real authority. Darnley became jealous of David Rizzio, the Queen's musician and secretary, and with a group of conspirators stabbed him to death in front of Mary when she was six months pregnant. After the birth of her son James, the future king, in Edinburgh Castle (she had him baptised a Catholic), Mary attempted a reconciliation with Darnley, yet she became attracted to James Hepburn, the Earl of Bothwell, some say even pregnant by him. In view of her estrangement with Darnley many suspected the child would not be his, yet Mary again tried reconciliation. It was during this period in **1567** that Darnley, recovering from an illness (possibly syphillis or smallpox) at nearby Kirk o'Field was found strangled, his body otherwise unmarked after a huge explosion in the house in which he was staying.

In **1567**, Mary married Bothwell in a Protestant ceremony after he was cleared of any connection with Darnley's murder. Their marriage ended one month later at Carberry, near Edinburgh, when Mary surrendered to a force of rebellious Protestant nobles under the Earl of Morton after a day of negotiation during which no blood was spilt. Mary abdicated and ultimately fled to England; she was subsequently executed on Queen Elizabeth I's command at Fotheringhay in **1587**.

In **1589** James VI married Anne, Princess of Denmark and, upon the death of Queen Elizabeth I of England in **1603**, became King of England, Scotland, Wales and Ireland as great-grandchild of James IV and great-great-grandchild of Henry VII of England. The Union of the Crowns was complete.

James was succeeded by his son Charles I (1625–1649), who believed, as his father had believed, in the Divine Right of Kings, and saw his principle duty towards Scotland as bringing the Scottish Kirk into line with the Church of England. In **1637** he attempted to foist his Church Service Book on the Scots. This led to a riot at St Giles' in Edinburgh and ultimately the drawing up and signing of the National Covenant, which disavowed the Divine Right of Kings in favour of man's duty to God. In **1640** the Scots marched into northern England, causing Charles to summon his first Parliament for ten years in order to raise funds to wage war on the Scots. Parliament, however, rebelled against the king, and in **1642** the Civil War began, with the Scottish Covenanters eventually joining Cromwell's Parliamentarians against the Royalists. A separate faction of Scots, under Montrose, joined the king's forces, but were defeated by David Leslie at Philiphaugh. Charles finally surrendered to the Scottish Army at Newark in **1646**, and was handed back to the Parliamentarians a year later, to be tried. He was executed in London in **1649**. A Commonwealth was established and Parliament declared it treason for anyone to be proclaimed king. However, his son, Charles II, was given the opportunity to be crowned King of Scotland, and this he accepted, at Scone in **1651**.

Cromwell's army marched north, and overthrew the Scots. Cromwell died in **1658** and by **1660** Charles II was restored to the throne, and set about putting down Presbyterianism in Scotland. The Covenanters opposed this but were finally defeated at Bothwell Bridge in **1679**. There then followed the persecutions under the Duke of York – known as 'The Killing Times'.

When Charles II died in **1685** he was succeeded by his brother James VII (of Scotland, James II of England) the first Roman Catholic monarch for well over a century, but one who was to reign for just three years, being deposed by his son-in-law, William of Orange, who was proclaimed William III of England and William II of Scotland. There were those in the Highlands, known as Jacobites, however, who still remained loyal to the legitimate king, James, and defeated William's forces sent against them at Killiecrankie in **1689**. But Jacobite resistance faded away, and the Highland Chieftans were forced to swear allegiance to William. When the MacDonalds of Glencoe refused in **1692**, they were massacred. In **1707**, under the reign of Queen Anne, the Act of Union was secured, the two kingdoms became Great Britain united under one Parliament. The Stuarts attempted to regain the throne from the now ruling House of Hanover, first in **1715** when an attempt to put the Old Pretender (son of James II) on the throne failed, and again in **1745** when Charles Edward Stuart, the Bonnie Prince, attempted to depose George II. After gathering together a small army, the Young Pretender enjoyed some initial success, but was finally routed at Culloden and his Jacobite army dispersed. Pursued by the king's forces, with a price of £30,000 on his head, he fled to the islands from where he hoped to escape to Scandinavia or France. Disguised as Betty Burke, a maid, he was brought from Benbecula to Kilbride Bay in Trotternish by Flora MacDonald, a 24-year-old Edinburgh-educated girl from Skye. After some close escapes, hiding in caves and cattle byres, he left Flora and went to Raasay the night after it had been sacked by troops from the Royal Navy ship *Furnace* as retribution against the men of the island who had supported the Jacobites. After a short stay, waiting for a French ship which never appeared, he went back to Skye, then on to Knoydart on the mainland. Finally, on 19 September **1746**, a French ship took him from Loch Nam Uamh, and he died in Rome in **1778**. Flora was arrested after his escape and held prisoner in a private house in London, but she was freed after the passing of the Indemnity Act in **1747**, when she became the heroine of London society.

The English, shaken by these events, set about destroying the clan system. The Disarming Act, which imposed severe penalties for carrying or possessing arms, or instruments of war, was enacted. These instruments were to include the kilt, tartan and the bagpipes. The Jacobite cause was finally lost. The history of the two countries merged, with Queen Victoria starting the now customary close association of the monarchy with Scotland.

Edinburgh People

Statue of Allan Ramsay

Edinburgh People

Edinburgh is a well-educated city with a long literary, artistic and scientific tradition. William Smellie, naturalist, antiquary, printer, contributor to the first edition of *Encyclopedia Brittanica*, and friend to many of the city's most notable 18thC figures wrote:

> 'In London, in Paris, and other large cities of Europe, though they contain literary men, the access to them is difficult; and even after that is obtained, the conversation is, for some time, shy and constrained. In Edinburgh, the access of men of parts is not only easy, but their conversation and the communication of their knowledge are at once imparted to intelligent strangers with the utmost liberality. They tell what they know, and deliver their sentiments without disguise or reserve.'

These traditions continue today with the work at the university and the hospitals, as well as the lively creative atmosphere of the Festival. Edinburgh, Stevenson's 'windy city' by the Forth, still has the power to inspire.

Robert Adam (1728–1792)
Architect, one of the four Scottish brothers. Known for his light and graceful neo-classical style, he was responsible for some of Edinburgh's finest architecture, such as Charlotte Square.

John Bartholomew (1890–1962)
One of the four generations of Bartholomews who have made such an outstanding contribution to cartography, he studied at Edinburgh University, as well as Paris and Leipzig. In the Gordon Highlanders during the First World War, he was mentioned in dispatches; later he worked on coding and deciphering. Honorary Secretary of the Royal Scottish Geographical Society for 30 years, he was presented with their Gold Medal and, as Cartographer Royal, was awarded a CBE in 1960. Bartholomew's offices are now at 12 Duncan Street.

Alexander Graham Bell (1847–1922)
Born at 16 South Charlotte Street, and educated at the Royal High School, his father was Professor of Elocution. This background, and his developing interest as a telegrapher, led to his invention of the telephone, while Professor of Vocal Physiology at Boston University, USA in 1876.

James Boswell (1740–1795)
Barrister, author and biographer of Dr Johnson, who he met in the Somerset Coffee House, 166 Strand, London, circa 1760. Buried in Auchinleck, his major works were *The Journal of a Tour of the Hebrides* (1744), *The Life of Samuel Johnson* (1791) and *Boswell's London Journal* (1762–63). He lived in Blair's Land, Parliament Square until he was nine years old, attended the High School and entered the university when he was 13. He had apartments in James Court, Lawnmarket and for a time rented 15a Meadow Place, the only one of his Edinburgh homes still standing.

Robert Burns (1759–1796)
Lionised as 'the heaven taught ploughman', Burns came to Edinburgh from Kilmarnock in 1786 after a journey of two days astride a borrowed pony. He lodged in Baxter's Close (now de-

molished, but see Lady Stair's Close) and following the success of the Kilmarnock edition of his poems set about making himself known in fashionable circles. The Edinburgh edition, printed by William Smellie, sold 3000 copies. He later returned to the city, staying in St James's Square in the New Town, to work on *Scots Musical Museum*, a song collection. It was then that he fell in love with Mrs Maclehose, 'Clarinda'. On his last visit to Edinburgh in November 1791, Burns stayed at the White Hart Inn, in the Grassmarket. The Burns memorial is in Regent Road and relics, including originals of some of his poems and the statue taken from his memorial, can be seen in Lady Stair's House.

Sir Arthur Conan Doyle (1859–1930)
Born in Edinburgh and studied medicine at the university. Dr Joseph Bell, one of his lecturers and a man with incredible powers of deduction, provided the inspiration for Sherlock Holmes. Conan Doyle gave up his medical practice in 1890 to devote himself to writing detective stories.

Robert Fergusson (1750–1774)
Born in Cap and Feather Close, which was demolished with the building of the North Bridge, he attended the High School, followed by Dundee Grammar School and finally four years at St Andrews University. In 1771 he became a regular contributor to *Ruddiman's Weekly Magazine*, and in 1773 his poems were published. Tragically he died of drink and madness in the city asylum at the age of 24. His best work, *The Farmer's Ingle*, became the model for Burn's *The Cotter's Saturday Night*. Burns felt indebted to Fergusson and, finding his grave in the Canongate churchyard neglected and overgrown, paid five pounds and ten shillings to have a stone erected.

Sir Patrick Geddes (1854–1932)
Described as 'the father of British town-planning', Geddes was born in Ballater and educated in Perth. A short time in banking was followed by a period studying botany in London and Paris. He was then appointed Lecturer in Zoology at Edinburgh University, even though he had no degree. He lived at 81a Princes Street, followed by 6 James Court in the Old Town and then Ramsay Lodge, at the foot of the Castle Esplanade. Geddes bought Short's observatory next door (now the Outlook Tower) and converted it into a 'sociological laboratory', arranged as an indexed museum of the universe. Visitors could see how Edinburgh related to Scotland, Scotland to Europe, Europe to the world and the earth to the solar system. He also demonstrated how environmental improvements could be made.

George Heriot (1563–1623)
Born in Edinburgh the son of a goldsmith, George Heriot followed in his father's footsteps, eventually setting up his own tiny shop in Parliament Close to the west of St Giles' Church. Appointed goldsmith to Anne of Denmark, wife of James VI, he began to amass a considerable fortune, such was the lady's passion for jewellery. In 1601 he received his greatest accolade, being appointed jeweller to the king, who he followed to London when James VI became King of England in 1603.

When he died, his will gave instructions that his fortune be used to found a school and hospital for the fatherless children and orphans of the burgesses and freemen of Edinburgh. 'Jinglin Geordie' established what is now George Heriot's School.

James Hogg (1770–1835)
The 'Ettrick Shepherd', who came to Edinburgh as the guest of Walter Scott in

1803, caused a sensation with his rough manners. A collector of Border ballads, he remained a life-long friend of Scott's, returning to Edinburgh several times and staying at the Harrow Inn, which was at 46–54 Candlemaker Row by the Grassmarket and later in Deanhaugh Street. His most remembered work is the frightening novel *The Private Memoirs and Confessions of a Justified Sinner* (1824).

David Hume (1711–1776)
Historian, humanitarian, philosopher, religious sceptic and leader in his time of the Edinburgh literati. Born and educated in the city, he owned his first home in Riddle's Close in the High Street, later moving to 229 Canongate, thence to James Court (destroyed by fire) and finally to a fine house which he built in the New Town, on the corner of St David Street and St Andrew Square. His tomb, designed by Robert Adam, stands in Calton Old Burial Ground. Once time keeper of the Advocates Library (1752), his major works were *Political Discourses* (1752) and *History of Great Britain* (1754–1761).

John Knox (1505–1572)
The great reformer was born near Haddington in East Lothian, and was a papal notary there from 1540–43, during which time he came to reject Roman Catholicism. He took over as Protestant Minister of St Andrews following the assassination of Cardinal Beaton in 1546, but was immediately captured by the French and held captive for two years until he was released by special request of Edward VI.

Following a period of self-imposed exile in Europe, Knox returned in 1559 to prepare the Confession of Faith, which denied the jurisdiction of Rome, and forbade mass. He was appointed minister of St Giles', and held this position until his death. In his life he did more than any other man to establish Protestantism, even to the extent of chastising Mary Queen of Scots regarding her Catholic religion. The house which bears his name at 45 High Street, in the Royal Mile, was probably his home only for the last few months of his life, when, as a sick man, his manse was deemed to be unsuitable.

Sir Harry Lauder (1870–1950)
The son of a potter, Harry Lauder was born at 3 Bridge Street, Portobello, in a humble single-storey cottage which was also home to his seven brothers and sisters. He learnt to sing and perform recitations with the Band of Hope in Arbroath while working as a flax-spinner, and through sheer determination became a professional music-hall entertainer in Glasgow in 1894. Dressed in tartan trousers he took London by storm in 1900, and seven years later he went on the first of his many visits to the USA, eventually becoming the most highly paid performer of his time.

Joseph Lister (1827–1921)
Although born in London, it was in Edinburgh that he pioneered the use of carbolic acid to reduce, dramatically, the incidence of post-operative infection. Having studied the writings of the great French chemist, Louis Pasteur, who had learnt that putrefaction was caused by air-borne organisms, Lister deduced that this could also cause the infection of wounds. His private practice in Edinburgh thrived, and he even attended Queen Victoria at Balmoral. He was presented with the Freedom of the City in 1898.

Lord George MacLeod of Fuinary (b 1895)
Minister of St Cuthbert's church, Princes Street, from 1926–1930, he founded the Iona Community in 1938 as a mission to help satisfy the spiritual needs of an industrial society. With six recently qual-

ified ministers, and six craftsmen, he set about rebuilding the ruined abbey. Iona now provides an important focus of spiritual regeneration. Half a million visitors come to the island each year.

John Menzies (1808–1879)

As befits Edinburgh's strong literary tradition, John Menzies was born in the city and educated at the Royal High School. He served his apprenticeship in a bookshop in the Calton district, starting work before eight in the morning to make the fire and sweep the pavement outside, and finishing at nine o'clock in the evening, six days a week, and with only New Year's Day as a holiday. There followed a time with Charles Tilt Booksellers in Fleet Street, London, until 1833 when his father died. He returned to Edinburgh and established his own shop at the corner of Princes Street and Hanover Street. The business flourished, expanding into station bookstalls. After his death the company continued to grow, going public in 1962. It is now a household name, with its head office in Hanover Buildings, Rose Street, and shops all over the country.

John Napier (1550–1617)

Born at Merchiston Castle in Edinburgh, and educated at St Andrews and Paris, he was a prodigious inventor, best known for his 20 years of work constructing the table of logarithms. Napier Polytechnic is named after him. His grave is in St Cuthbert's churchyard.

James Nasmyth (1808–1890)

Born in Edinburgh, Nasmyth was the pioneer of the motor car, having succeeded in propelling a steam driven carriage and eight passengers along the Queensferry Road. His other achievements included the designing of the steam-hammer, the steam pile-driver and a hydraulic punching machine.

Henry Raeburn (1756–1823)

Educated at Heriot's Hospital and apprenticed to a goldsmith, Raeburn became Scotland's best known 18thC painter. He worked from a studio in George Street from 1787 and was knighted by George IV at Hopetoun House in 1822. His works hang in the National Gallery of Scotland – look out for the picture of the Reverend Robert Walker skating, it is particularly amusing.

Allan Ramsay (1686–1758)

A wig-maker's apprentice who came to the city in 1701 and became one of its best known poets and booksellers, opening his shop 'at the sign of the Mercury, opposite the head of Niddry's Wynd' in 1718. Here he compiled a collection of Scottish songs, *The Tea Table Miscellany* (1724–32) and wrote his most famous work *The Gentle Shepherd* (1725). In 1726 he took a new shop in the Luckenbooths (by St Giles', now gone) and two years later started Scotland's first lending library, with a store of some 30,000 books. It was frowned upon by the Calvinists, who declared the volumes 'profane and obscene'. He retired to an eccentric octagonal house on Castle Hill, nicknamed 'Goose Pie', which is now barely recognisable amidst the picturesque pile of Ramsay Gardens. Buried in London there is a memorial to him at Greyfriars.

Sir Walter Scott (1771–1832)

Born on 15 August in a house near 8 Chambers Street, his family moved to 25 George Square in 1774 and stayed until 1797. Scott was a sickly child, who spent much of his childhood in bed, reading romantic novels and poetry. He attended the High School and university, qualifying as an advocate in 1792. Married to Charlotte Carpenter in 1797, they lodged at 108 George Street, and then at 10 South Castle Street, before setting up home for 28 years at 39 Castle Street – look for the statuette above the door. It was here that Scott, certainly one of Scotland's best loved writers, would work, accompanied by his faithful hound Maida, and an old tom cat. Most of the Waverley novels were written here – in one frantic period he wrote two volumes in three weeks. Following the crash of Ballantyne's bookselling business, in which Scott was a partner, he lodged at various addresses in the city, finally retiring to Abbotsford in 1812 and stayed there until his death. He is buried in Dryburgh Abbey; the magnificent Scott monument stands in Princes Street. Among the list of his distinguished works are *Heart of Midlithian* (1818), *Ivanhoe* (1819) and *Betrothed* (1825).

Sir James Young Simpson (1811–1870)

After studying at Edinburgh University he was appointed Professor of Midwifery in 1839 and can be said to be the originator of the modern practice of gynaecology. He is, however, best known as the discoverer of the value of chloroform as an anaesthetic in 1847. He inspired such confidence that Queen Victoria agreed to the use of it at the birth of Prince Leopold in 1853.

Tobias Smollett (1721–1771)

A contemporary of David Hume, he described Edinburgh's literary society as 'a hotbed of genius'. He lived for a while at 22 St John Street, and is best remembered for his descriptive novel *Humphrey Clinker* (1771).

Muriel Spark (b 1918)

Born and educated in Edinburgh, her novel *The Prime of Miss Jean Brodie* typified life as it may have been during her schooldays – at James Gillespie's School for Girls (now merged with the boys school) in Warrender Park Road, to the south of Bruntsfield Links.

Robert Louis Stevenson (1850–1894)

Baptised Robert Louis Balfour (after his maternal grandfather), Stevenson was born at 8 Howard Place, opposite the Royal Botanic Gardens, and moved at the age of seven to 17 Heriot Row in the northern New Town. A sickly child and a not particularly healthy adult, he spent much time in the sunshine of the South Pacific, but always returned to Heriot Row, which was to be his home for 30 years. Most of his childhood was spent in the company of his much loved nurse, Alison Cunningham ('his first wife and second mother'), to whom he dedicated *A Child's Garden of Verses*. Although his school attendance was erratic due to poor health, he entered the university in 1867 and qualified as an advocate, having originally entered as an engineering student at his father's wish. He gradually turned to literature as a career, and wrote many popular masterpieces, including his most famous, *Treasure Island* (1883) and *The Strange Case of Dr Jekyll and Mr Hyde* (1886). *Kidnapped* (1886) and its sequel *Catriona* (1893) are two other exciting tales. He also wrote the lovely *Skye Boat Song*. Relics can be seen at Lady Stair's House.

James Watt (1736–1819)

Not the inventor of the steam engine as is widely thought but the man who harnessed its efficient use. Although he worked mainly in Glasgow and London, he was a frequent visitor to Edinburgh and was elected a Fellow of the Royal Society of Edinburgh in 1784. In 1852, the Edinburgh School of Arts became the Watt Institution in recognition of his work, and was amalgamated as the present Heriot-Watt College three years later. Watt's bronze statue has stood in Chambers Street since 1854.

Edinburgh Castle

The Castle is as potent a symbol of Scotland as the thistle or the pipes. In a theatrical position on top of the crag, it dominates the city which has grown up around it.

The crag, on which the Castle stands, was left exposed by an Ice Age glacier, which carved the valleys now occupied by the Grassmarket and Princes Street Gardens some 83m below. The hard basaltic core of an extinct volcano, the crag (also known as Castle Rock) resisted the gouging of the ice in a way that the softer surrounding material could not. A ridge was also left by the glacier in a gentle slope to the east of the crag, the spine of which is now occupied by the Royal Mile.

Although King Mynyddog is known to have feasted in the hall of 'Din Eidyn' in the 6thC, a clear picture of the Castle can only be drawn from the 11thC. When St Margaret, Queen of Scotland, died in 1093 there were walls defending the royal residence, oratory and church which were built on the summit. The oldest surviving building within the Castle, a chapel dedicated to St Margaret, now occupies part of this site. It was well described by John Taylor, Thames waterman and poet, who walked to Scotland in 1618. He wrote in his *Pennyles Pilgrimage*, 'the Castle on a loftie rocke is so strongly grounded, bounded and founded, that by force of man it can never be confounded'.

The following chronology illustrates the Castle's turbulent development from fortified royal residence to military stronghold and finally national monument.

1093	Donald Bane, king from 1093–7, attacks Castle. Queen Margaret dies.
1296–	Castle changes hands four times during the Wars of Indepen-
1341	dence. Defences dismantled.
1356	Released from captivity, David II begins a rebuilding programme which is to be continued for the following 200 years.
1361	New well sunk and defensive tower, the Wellhouse Tower, built to guard it.
1377	David's Tower, the new royal residence, built.
1379	New Gate Tower and Constables Tower finished.
1435	King's Great Chamber built during the reign of James I (and rebuilt following seige of 1445).
1511	Great Hall completed.
1540	Register House built.
1542	James V dies and Palace of Holyroodhouse supercedes Castle as the royal residence, which is assuming an increasingly military

role. The Old Hall becomes an arsenal, a House of Artillery is put up, and St Mary's Church converted to a store for munitions. The Castle is now the most important stronghold in Scotland, and the state records are moved here.

1544   Earl of Hertford sacks Edinburgh but does not seriously threaten the Castle. Following this the defences are again strengthened.

1566   Mary Queen of Scots gives birth to James in a small room in the Castle on 19 June. An isolated and symbolic gesture, since the Castle is seen to represent the Scottish Crown.

1573   Castle captured by the Earl of Morton, aided by English artillery; severe damage inflicted. Much rebuilding over next 15 years, including The Half Moon Battery and Portcullis Gate.

1640   Castle taken by Covenanters under General Leslie after a three month siege. Again badly damaged, and once more repaired.

1650   Cromwell occupies Castle after three months siege. Castle now used as barracks.

1689   Siege by forces of William and Mary, followed by repair and further strengthening.

1737   Whole of south and west perimeter wall rebuilt.

1742   Dry ditch across eastern approach, begun during Cromwell's occupation, completed.

1745   Last military action against Castle, when the forces of Charles Edward Stuart, the Young Pretender, make a half-hearted attempt to take it.

1755   St Mary's Church demolished. New Ordnance Store built.

1757   Castle houses French prisoners of war until 1814.

1799   New barracks completed to house soldiers fighting the French.

1816   Esplanade finished.

1818   The Honours of Scotland discovered in a chest, where they had lain since the Act of Union in 1707. The Castle is now seen as a national monument.

1845   A storehouse is identified as being St Margaret's Chapel, and is restored in 1852.

1861   One o'clock gun fired for the first time.

1863   North Barracks reconstructed.

1886   Portcullis Gate remodelled.

1891   Great Hall renovated.

1896   Ordnance Stores converted into a hospital.

1927   Scottish National War Memorial completed. The Castle now stands as we see it today.

Edinburgh Castle

Castle open Apr–Sep 09.30–17.05 Mon–Sat; 10.00–17.05 Sun. Oct–Mar 09.00–16.20 Mon–Sat; 12.30–15.35 Sun. 031–225 9841. Admission charge. Guided tours.

The following descriptions of the various Castle buildings are arranged as far as possible in the form of a tour, climbing up Hawk Hill and returning via the Lang Stairs.

Esplanade

Completed in its present form in 1816, it measures about 130 × 90m and is used for various ceremonials and parades, and annually in August for the Royal Military Tattoo. Prior to its building the approach to the Castle was naturally much steeper, and more defensible. There is a row of suitably military monuments on the north side. It is interesting to note that part of the Esplanade, just to the right of the Castle entrance, is the territory of Nova Scotia. A decree by Charles I was never cancelled, and a plaque records this fact.

Gatehouse

Built 1882–8 and with no strategic pretence, it makes for a rather timid entrance compared to the sturdier stuff beyond the drawbridge (which was, incidentally, the last to be built in Scotland). Robert Lorimer added the niches which flank the archway in 1929. The statues in the niches are, to the left, Robert the Bruce who defeated the English led by Edward II at Bannockburn in 1314 and thus regained Scotland's independence and, to the right, William Wallace, who led the revolt against Edward I and defeated the English at Stirling Bridge in 1297. Both statues were unveiled in 1929, the 600th anniversary of the city's oldest surviving charter, granted by Bruce in 1329. They were sculpted by Thomas Clapperton and Alexander Carrick respectively. Gateway surmounted by Royal Arms of Scotland.

Portcullis Gate

The initial stage was completed in 1577 on the site of Constable's Tower, destroyed when the English captured the Castle in 1573. The original portcullis, open to the elements, quickly rusted away, so in 1584 another two storeys were added to house both the portcullis and the Captain of the Castle. The flat roof served as a gun emplacement. In 1867 it was rebuilt to resemble as closely as possible the original 14thC Constable's Tower. The present portcullis, decorative rather than defensive, is protected by two outer doors and an inner door. The 9th Earl of Argyll was held here prior to his execution in 1688 – so it is sometimes referred to as the Argyll Tower.

Argyll Battery

Named after the 2nd Duke of Argyll, Commander-in-chief of Scotland, who fought the Jacobites at Sheriffmuir in 1715, the battery consists of six 18thC muzzle-loaders. It was built in 1730 for Major General Wade, of military roads and bridges fame.

Mills Mount Battery

Beyond the Argyll Battery, and originally overlooking an area of open fields beyond Nor' Loch. It now affords splendid views of Princes Street and the 18thC New Town. It is from here that the one o'clock gun is fired each weekday, a custom initiated in 1861 to serve as a time signal for ships in the Forth. It is now fired by an electronic device controlled

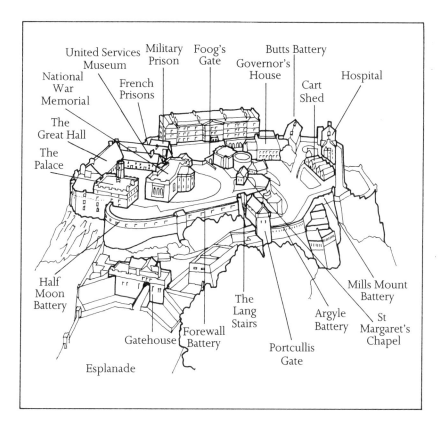

National War Memorial · United Services Museum · Military Prison · Foog's Gate · Butts Battery · Governor's House · French Prisons · Cart Shed · Hospital · The Great Hall · The Palace · Half Moon Battery · The Lang Stairs · Mills Mount Battery · Gatehouse · Forewall Battery · Argyle Battery · St Margaret's Chapel · Portcullis Gate · Esplanade

from the Royal Observatory. Below the Mill's Mount Battery is the **Low Defence,** dating from around 1540. This once served as the Governor's Garden.

Further round, behind the Hospital (see below) are the **Western Defences,** which date from the 17thC. The present upper terrace dates from 1858.

Cart Shed

An 18thC building, used also as a barracks and an ordnance store. It is now a tea room.

Hospital

A handsome building with crow-stepped gables, converted from the old

ordnance stores in 1896, during the great period of remodelling and improving. Not open to the public.

Butts Battery

Built in 1708–13 to strengthen the defences in response to fears of revolt against the Act of Union. Indeed a squadron of French ships had sailed up the Forth in 1708 in support of the Old Pretender (the son of James II). The bow butts, where archers practised, used to be in this area.

Governor's House

Erected in 1742, it is both sturdy and classical, supported on either side by

23

wings which once housed the Master Gunner and Store-Keeper. The main building is now the Officers' Mess, the Governor now occupying the right wing. Not open to the public.

Military Prison

Built circa 1842 to accommodate prisoners from all Scottish units, its cells, although spartan, could be centrally heated. Externally, its handsome design reflects the thought that was given to the Castle buildings at that time. The last inmates left in 1923.

French Prisons

The vaults which were built to support the Great Hall have, over the years, been used variously for stores, munitions, barracks and even as a bakehouse. But most notable of their uses was as dungeons during the wars with the French from the mid 1700s until the end of the Napoleonic Wars in 1815. Graffiti made on the stones by the inmates can still be seen, (especially at the main entrance), as can some very fine models they made to pass away the time, displayed in the Scottish United Services Museum (see below).

Mons Meg

This magnificent siege cannon, 'the lass wi' the iron mou' ('mou' meaning mouth), dating from circa 1440, is now kept in the vaults of the French Prison, away from the ravages of the elements. It was manufactured for the Duke of Burgundy and given to James II, his nephew by marriage, in 1457. Its cannonballs, each weighing 150kg, could be fired at targets over 1600m away. Having seen action, it finally burst while firing a salute for the Duke of York in 1682. After a period on display at the Tower of London, it was returned here in 1829, a symbol of Scottish patriotism.

Dury's Battery

Commanding the southern approach to the Castle, these defences are named after Theodore Dury, who rebuilt the southern wall 1708–13.

Foog's Gate

At the top of Hawk Hill and facing the vast Barrack Block, Foog's Gate was built to provide access to the upper enclosure near the highest point on Castle Rock. It probably dates from the reign of Charles II (1660–1685), and is ingeniously sited in order that guns in the neighbouring wall can protect it. Prior to its construction, the entrance to this inner enclosure was via the Lang Stairs. The origin of the name Foog is not known.

The Forewall and Half Moon Batteries

The Forewall Battery follows the original line of the Castle's eastern defences, and from this elevated position gives a wide range of fire to protect the Castle entrance. Similarly, the Half Moon Battery was built following the siege of 1573 and gave excellent cover over and beyond the area now occupied by the Esplanade. The actual level of these batteries is that of the summit of the crag – they are supported on the remains of David's Tower and a series of vaults, which, at one time, were used as a reservoir for the Castle. The view over the Old Town is superb from here.

The Palace

This occupies the site of earlier 15thC Royal accommodation, but the present building is mainly 16thC – a stone above one of the doors, with the initials MAH (Mary Queen of Scots and Henry Lord Darnley), is dated 1566. The palace was modelled in 1617 for James VI, when the pattern of windows was regularised to conform with the classical taste of the time. The last major work was the heightening of the octagonal stair turret in 1820 with a grotesque extension topped by a flagstaff.

Inside is the small **bed chamber,** where Mary Queen of Scots gave birth to James (later James VI) in 1566 and which was later redecorated for James himself. One side of the room looks out onto the Grassmarket and a tradition exists that the infant James was lowered out of this window in a basket to be smuggled to safety, and possibly to be baptised in his mother's faith.

The **Honours of Scotland** – crown, sword and sceptre – were kept in the Crown Chamber above Mary's rooms. The crown, of Scottish gold, began as a circlet for Robert the Bruce at the end of the Wars of Succession. It was remodelled by James V and received a new bonnet and ermine for Queen Elizabeth II in 1953. The sceptre is 16thC and the sword was presented to James IV in 1507 by Pope Julius. It bears the oak leaves and acorns, emblem of the Pope and the Stuarts. They were hidden in a chest at the time of Cromwell's occupation in Scotland and walled in after the Act of Union in 1707. They came to light in 1817 when a commission, on which Sir Walter Scott served, discovered them.

The Great Hall

Occupying the south side of Crown Square, the present Great Hall (for there have been several) dates from the 6thC. During the early Middle Ages a hall such as this would have served as a communal living space for all the household, but this gradually changed, until its main function was to accommodate great ceremonial occasions. It was for this purpose that James IV built the hall, extending the space available by building the massive sub-structure now known as the French Prisons. Around 1650 it was converted for use as barracks, being partitioned with walls and floors. Later it served as a hospital.

It was Thomas Nelson, the publisher, who provided funds for its renovation from 1887–91 and Hippolyte Blanc who prepared the designs, which owe more to his imagination than historic fact. But one should not disparage his work, for this is surely most people's idea of what a great hall should be.

A wooden partition separates the doorway from the main body of the Hall, a device to avoid draughts. Fine wood panelling, displays of weapons and suits of armour adorn the walls. The hammerbeam roof, although altered, contains much that is original, and is thought to be the work of John Drum-

St Margaret's Chapel

The oldest building within the Castle walls, occupying the highest point on the crag. It dates from the early 12thC, and was most probably built during the reign of David I, some time after 1124. A tall rectangular building with only five small windows, it was re-discovered in 1845 after being used as a store and powder magazine for many years. Sensitively restored, the interior is particularly charming; it is divided into two halves by

a curved, finely decorated chancel arch, beautiful in its simplicity, with space today for only 26 worshippers. The stained glass windows by Douglas Strachan, 1922, depict William Wallace and the saints Andrew, Columba, Margaret and Ninian in bright glowing colours. Just below the chapel is the pets' cemetery, where miniature gravestones mark the last resting places of the officers' dogs.

mond, the king's principal carpenter. The uniformity of girth of the timbers, and the absence of any massive beams does, however, result in a lack of drama. The intricately patterned painting, crests and scrolls, is some compensation.

At the far end is a large fireplace, a modern creation based on a 15thC design at Borthwick in Lothian. The Great Hall should not be missed.

Scottish United Services Museum

Military memorabilia and artefacts and the story of the Scottish Soldier 1600–1914 exhibition, in what were once officers quarters. It was built in 1708 on the site of minor buildings, kitchens and the like, which served the Great Hall. Converted into a museum in 1930, it stands upon part of the vaults now known as the French Prisons.

The Scottish National War Memorial

The most modern of the Castle buildings, and a touching memorial to Scotland's dead in the First World War. The original building on this site was the church of St Mary, used during the 16thC to store munitions and later de-molished to make way for a barrack block, erected in 1755. It was upon the shell of this building that Sir Robert Lorimer designed the Memorial, which was opened by the Prince of Wales in 1927.

Lorimer's major external alterations included an elaborate entrance and an octagonal apse enclosing the very summit of Castle Rock, 'the centre round which Scottish history, in all its rugged and varied picturesqueness, has revolved'. Inside, the pillared Hall of Valour displays flags, memorials and a frieze commemorating battle fields of the First World War, lit by stained glass by Douglas Strachan. Opposite the entrance is the shrine, protected by wrought iron gates topped with thistles, where a casket containing a record of those killed is prominently displayed. The richness of the interior contrasts with the subdued exterior, which blends in with the earlier buildings close by.

The Lang Stairs

A steep flight which was the main means of entry to the important inner Castle during the Middle Ages. It adjoins the upper storeys of the Portcullis Gate.

The Royal Mile

St Giles' Cathedral

Sloping gently from the Castle to the Palace of Holyroodhouse, the Royal Mile is a crowded, historic and romantic jumble of buildings from past centuries. Straddling the crest of a ridge to the east of the Castle crag it stretches for a lang Scots mile (1984 yards), divided into four contiguous parts: Castlehill, Lawnmarket, High Street and Canongate.

There was certainly some kind of fortification on Castle Rock in the 6thC, and as this became more significant, a cluster of cottages were built close to the Castle gate, at the top of what is now the High Street and Lawnmarket. It was David I who founded the Royal Burgh of Edinburgh. He decided that some order should be brought to the town by dividing the land on either side of the High Street into 'tofts', narrow strips upon which each citizen was to build a dwelling within a year and a day. In 1376 the population had risen to about 2000, and subsequent division of the tofts created forelands (a 'land' being a building) and backlands. They were reached through a narrow close between the forelands or through a pend, or archway, when the buildings actually joined.

In this way the High Street rapidly became built up, as did Canongate, a separate burgh founded by the canons of Holyrood in 1140, which was to remain independent of the city until 1856. Further expansion of the population increased pressure on the space available within the city walls, until the only way left to build was up, and to create the suburbs of Cowgate and Grassmarket. Limited water supply and lack of provision for proper sanitation brought conditions of unimaginable squalor to the city's seething spine.

In 1544, during a period known as the 'Rough Wooing', Henry VIII demanded that Mary Queen of Scots (then three years old) should marry his son Edward, to gain support of the Scottish Lords. An English army, led by the Earl of Hertford, burned their way up the Royal Mile from the Palace of Holyroodhouse, and laid waste to everything else within a seven mile radius. This was inevitably followed by a great rebuilding, with stone replacing wood, slate replacing thatch, and the amalgamation of tofts to accommodate courts enclosed by tenements.

In the 18thC the population crammed within the city walls was some 50,000. The appalling conditions led to crime and disease which reached epidemic proportions. It was graphically described by Daniel Defoe in his *Tour thro' the Whole Island of Great Britain*:

'In a Morning, earlier than seven o'clock, before the human Excrements are swept away from the doors, it stinks intolerably; for, after Ten at Night, you run a great Risque, if you walk the Streets, of having Chamberpots of Ordure thrown upon your Head: and it sounds very oddly in the Ears of a Stranger, to hear all Passers-by cry out, as loud as to be heard to the uppermost Storeys of the House, which are generally six or seven high in the Front of the High Street, 'Hoad yare Hoand'; that is 'Hold your Hand' and throw not, till I am passed.'

It was Lord Provost George Drummond who provided, shortly after his appointment in 1725, the impetus for building the New Town to the north of the existing city. When building began some 50 years later, after Drummond's death, the wealthier sections of the community abandoned the Old Town in favour of the New. With only the poor left, the Royal Mile soon became an area of slums.

On the night of 15 November 1824 a great fire broke out in a tenement at the top of Old Assembly Close. It rapidly spread along the south side of the High Street to the Exchequer Buildings, destroying everything in its wake. When it was thought the fire had been doused, the Tron Kirk was discovered to be alight. The wood and lead tower burned fiercely before collapsing in a shower of sparks and molten metal. Miraculously, the body of the church was saved.

Improvement Acts in 1827 and 1867 provided for the renovation of the slums and replacement of some of the narrow closes with 10 new streets. Life improved, but it was to be many years before the fashionable returned. During the 1930s Canongate was largely rebuilt, but unfortunately much of its original character was lost in the process. The flags, poles extending over the street on which the washing was dried, disappeared as did the last vestiges of the slums. It has only been in the more recent past that restoration and rebuilding has been executed with sympathy for the original architectural concepts, and the results are the many handsome buildings we see today – Chessell's Court, Bible Lands, Wardrop's Court and many others.

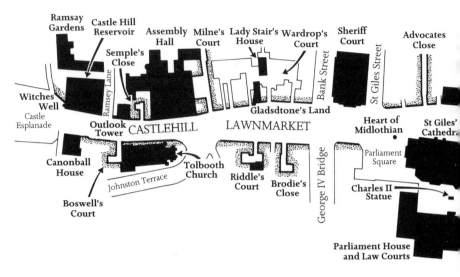

North Side
Downhill towards Holyrood

Castle Hill Reservoir
Rebuilt 1849–50 on the site of Edinburgh's first reservoir, which was built in 1720 and held water piped from Comiston Springs, some five miles to the south. This fed five cisterns in the High Street. The present squat, dour construction supplies a wider area, and holds 8.5 million litres.

Witches Well
A cast iron fountain, fixed to the south west corner of the reservoir, marks the spot where over 300 unfortunate women, thought to be witches, were cruelly put to death while the righteous looked on. It all happened between 1479 and 1722 and as you would imagine, the charges laid against the so called witches were unbelievable. For example, Dame Euphane MacCalzean

was found guilty of using a spell to sink a vessel out of Leith, and trying to destroy King James VI's ship as it entered North Berwick. Agnes Fynnie was burnt in 1643 after 'depriving 12 people of their speech'. In court the women were stripped to the waist 'and if the Devil's marks are seen that is proof that Satan has nipped her person'. The most incredible case was that of Major Thomas Weir who, in 1670, was hanged in the Grassmarket as a witch – part of the evidence against him was given by a beggar who claimed to have seen Weir riding along the High Street in a coach accompanied by the Devil.

Ramsay Gardens
Incorporating the eccentric octagonal house, nicknamed 'Goose Pie', which poet and publisher Allan Ramsay (1686–1758) built for himself, this inventive example of early town planning was built by Professor Patrick Geddes as a hall of residence and flats 1892–4. Seen from Princes Street, it perches below the

The Royal Mile

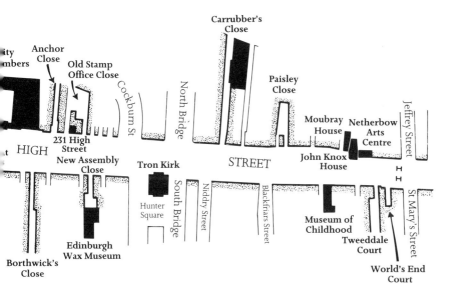

Castle like some grand and extravagant folly.

Outlook Tower

031–226 3709. Reconstructed from a 17thC tenement building in 1853 as Short's Observatory, by the optician Maria Theresa Short. It was purchased in 1892 by Professor Patrick Geddes who created a teaching museum, or 'sociological laboratory', here. This no longer survives, and the lens and mirror of the original camera obscura were replaced in 1945 with a superior system which, on a clear day, projects a panorama of the City of Edinburgh onto a white concave table to the accompaniment of an informed commentary. It is a good introduction to the city, and a must if your time is limited. There are fine views from the roof top terrace, a history of the camera obscura, a display of holograms and an exhibition of pin-hole photographs – taken with biscuit tins and drink cans. *Open 10.00–17.00 Mon–Fri; 10.00–16.00 Sat & Sun. Admission charge.*

Semple's Close

A 17thC mansion with inscribed door lintels, dated 1638. Lady Sempill, the widow of the eighth Lord Sempill, lived here.

Assembly Hall

Built by David Bryce in 1859 on the site of the Palace of Mary of Guise, mother of Mary Queen of Scots, this is where the General Assembly of the Church of Scotland holds its annual meeting. It is the back of this-dull Gothic building which faces Castlehill.

Milne's Court

Robert Mylne's 1690 attempt at open plan design amidst the crowded closes of the Old Town. He built a courtyard enclosed by existing buildings on the east and west and which is now part of the University Halls of Residence. In 1971 it won the Saltaire Society award for reconstruction. **James' Court,** to the east, is a later copy by James Brownhill. David Hume (1711–1776), philosopher and historian, lived here, as did James Boswell (1740–1795), who chronicled the life of the poet, Dr Johnson.

Gladstone's Land
031–226 5856. When Thomas Gledstanes bought a 16thC building from the Fisher family on 20 December 1617, he initiated a rebuilding programme which survives substantially as we see it today. A curved forestair stands beside an arcaded front, enclosing reconstructed shop booths, with round pillars supporting a typically narrow frontage some five storeys tall, culminating in two equal gables. Presented to the National Trust for Scotland by Miss Helen Harrison in 1934, it was sensitively restored by Sir Frank Mears and Robert Hurd. The renovations exposed some splendid original work – of particular note is the 17thC painting in the first floor front room. Owned by the Gledstanes until well into the 18thC, it remains a superb example of a 17thC town house. *Guided tours if pre-booked. Open Apr–Oct 10.00–17.00 Mon–Sat; 14.00–17.00 Sun; Nov, 10.00–16.30 Sat; 14.00–16.30 Sun. Closed Dec–Mar. Admission charge.*

There is also a gallery featuring a changing exhibition of contemporary work open from *Mar–Oct* and a textile workshop *open 10.00–17.00 Mon–Fri.*

Lady Stair's House
Lady Stair's Close. 031–225 2424 x 6593. Built in 1622 for Sir William Grey of Pittendrum and purchased in 1719 by Elizabeth, Dowager Countess of Stair, it was sold to the fifth Earl of Rosebery in 1893, enthusiastically restored by George S. Aitken in 1897, and presented to the city in 1907. Note the carving on the lintel over the entrance door, which is inscribed with the initials of Sir William Grey and his wife, and bears the date 1622. Inside you will find period room settings, and collections of

memorabilia relating to the lives and works of Burns, Scott and Stevenson. Indeed Robert Burns came to Edinburgh in 1786, and lodged in nearby Baxter's Close, long since demolished. *Open Oct–May 10.00–17.00 Mon–Sat; June–Sep 10.00–18.00 Mon–Sat and 14.00–17.00 on Suns during the Festival. Admission free.*

Wardrop's Court
Adjoining Lady Stair's Close and entered through an archway guarded by four iron dragons. Wardrop's Court was formed when two smaller closes were demolished in the 1840s.

Sheriff Court
A dour neo-Georgian edifice completed in 1937. The main criminal court is here, but not the High Court.

Advocates Close
Down several flights of steps to Market Street, it is worth exploring to examine two fine door lintels in a tenement, built in 1590. One is inscribed *Blissit be God of al his gifts*; the other, *Spes altera vitae 1590*. It was once the house of Sir James Stewart of Goodtrees, Lord Advocate of Scotland 1692–1709 and 1711–13. Set back on the opposite side of the close is a house named after Bishop Adam Bothwell, built circa 1630.

City Chambers
A decorated 18thC building designed by John Adam, enclosing a courtyard on three sides and entered from the High Street through a single-storey arcaded screen. Completed in 1761 it incorporated shops, coffee houses, printing presses, flats and a covered merchants' exchange – the merchants, however, had other ideas and continued to trade on the street as was customary. The Council first established their City Chambers here in 1811, and finally took over the whole building in 1893, ex-

tending it in 1901. The City of Edinburgh District Council, its 64 members chaired by the Lord Provost, meet here with other council business being conducted in the adjoining offices; this extensive accommodation can be seen from Cockburn Street, where the rear of the building stands fully 12 storeys tall. The statue in the forecourt is of Alexander training his horse Brucephalus. Modelled in 1832, it was cast in 1883 and moved to its present position in 1916, after standing in St Andrew Square. Prior to the building of the City Chambers, Sir Simon Preston of Craigmillar, Provost of the City of Edinburgh 1566–7, lodged in a building on this site. On 15 June 1567 Mary Queen of Scots spent her last night in Edinburgh here, after her surrender to the Confederate Lords at Carberry Hill. She was then taken to Holyrood and from there to Loch Leven Castle as a state prisoner. After escaping and fleeing to England she was imprisoned by Queen Elizabeth and beheaded at Fotheringhay Castle in 1587.

Anchor Close

Of historical rather than architectural interest, this was the site of the Anchor Tavern and the nearby printing works of William Smellie, who produced the first edition of the *Encyclopaedia Brittanica* here in 1768, as well as works by Robert Burns, in 1787. Indeed it was Smellie who introduced Burns into the Crochallan Fencibles, a drinking club which met in the tavern. Of Smellie, Burns wrote:

'His uncomb'd grizzly locks wild staring, thatche'd
A head for thought profound and clear, unmatch'd;
Yet, tho' his caustic wit was biting rude,
His heart was warm, benevolent, and good.'

The close was also the home of Sir Walter Scott's parents until 1771.

231 High Street

Now an Italian restaurant, it was once James Gillespie's snuff shop. Its success enabled him to bequeath enough money to the Edinburgh Merchant Company for the founding of the now famous Gillespie school.

Old Stamp Office Close

An attractive close, home of the Scottish Inland Revenue between 1779–1821,

Mary King's Close

If you go into Cockburn Street, you will find a barred gate leading to the remains of the saddest close of all, built into the side of the City Chambers. It was here that the death toll from the Great Plague was greatest, such that the city magistrates ordered it sealed off. It remained crumbling and empty until the shortage of accommodation forced a few hapless families to take up residence, but it was not long before a series of ghostly apparitions caused them to flee in terror. After fire damage in 1750 what we can see today, a recognisable series of doorways rising part way to the High Street, was incorporated into the Royal Exchange, now the City Chambers. Apparently, in one of the rooms, hooks embedded in the ceiling suggest it was used as a butcher's shop. One can visit the buried street, which runs under the City Chambers by applying in writing to Edinburgh District Council. Unfortunately there is a long waiting list.

and also the fashionable Fortune's Tavern, where the Lord High Commissioner to the Church of Scotland held receptions. Flora MacDonald, heroine of Charles Edward Stuart's flight after the unsuccessful '45 rebellion, went to school here, so it is quite fitting that the close now houses the Royal Mile Nursery.

Carrubber's Close
A walk down the close, past the House of Archbishop Spottiswood (1578, rebuilt 1864) will bring you to Old St Paul's Episcopal Church, its bellcote silhouetted against the sky but the rest of the building is well and truly hemmed in. Originally a wool store, it was occupied by Alexander Rose, Bishop of Edinburgh and his congregation after their expulsion from St Giles' in 1689, and soon became a Jacobite stronghold. In 1880 a new building was begun on the site of the old, which had become ruinous, and continued in stages which culminated in the building of the Warriors' Chapel in 1924. The interior stonework and contrasting levels are quite dramatic, and rich furnishings are particularly notable – especially the altar, the triptych which contains figures by Sebastian Zwink of Oberammergau, and a sculpture of the Madonna and Child by Louis Deuchars.

Paisley Close
A carved portrait above the entrance bears the inscription *Heave awa' chaps, I'm no' dead yet*, which refers to the rescue of one boy trapped in the debris when a tenement collapsed in 1861, killing 35 occupants.

Moubray House
Although the frontage was rebuilt circa 1630, parts of Moubray House date from the early 15thC. Note the characteristic outside stair. Daniel Defoe edited the *Edinburgh Courant* from this building in 1710. The 19thC ground floor shop now sells knitwear, and outside is the old Fountain Well.

John Knox House
031–556 6961. John Knox was converted from Catholicism in 1542 and became the leader of the Reformers in Scotland. Imprisoned by the French for two years in revenge for the murder of Cardinal Beaton, he returned to Scotland and did more than any other man to establish Protestantism, even to the extent of chastising Mary Queen of Scots regarding her Roman Catholic religion and light-heartedness. Forced to take refuge in England, he returned to Scotland and continued preaching until his death in November 1572. It was only in August of that same year, when he was a sick man, that he stayed here with Mossman, his own manse being unsuitable for a dying man. The house is quite astonishingly picturesque, and dates from the late 15thC. Built from polished freestone with an outside stairway, it was probably extended in either 1525 or 1544, and remains a prime example of the once common overhanging wooden upper floors with crow-stepped gables. Its original occupants were the Arres family, who lived there until Mariota Arres' husband, James Mossman, became Assaye of the Mint to Mary Queen of Scots, and moved to the Castle. Shops have always occupied the ground floor and basement – wigmakers, painters, fishmongers and others.

The interiors: the Oak Room with its original fireplace and 16thC wall painting, and the study, are evocative of life in the 15thC and 16thC. There is a gift shop and coffee house. Exterior decorations include a prominent inscription which reads *Lufe God abufe al and yi nychtbour as yi self* (Love God above all and thy neighbour as thy self), a garlanded coat of arms bearing the initials of James Mossman and Mariotta Arres, and a sundial with a carved relief of Moses. This latter item once incorporated a model pulpit and effigy of John Knox – this can now be seen in the museum inside. *Open Apr–Oct 10.00–17.00 Mon–Sat; Nov–Mar 10.00–16.00 Mon–Sat. Admission charge.*

Netherbow Arts Centre
The name recalls the old Netherbow Port, the main eastern city gate built in 1513 and demolished in 1764. Studs in the road indicate its actual position, and the old bell which hung in this spired building is preserved in the Arts Centre, which features changing exhibitions of contemporary work.

Morocco Land
On the front of this lively modern development is the half length effigy of a Moor, recalling the earlier tenement building occupied by Andrew Gray, who made his fortune in Morocco.

Bible Land
An extensively restored 17thC tenement built by the Incorporation of Cordwainers, or Shoemakers, and so called because of the fine stone plaque above the entrance door. Dated 1677, the inscription reads:
Behold how good a thing it is and how becoming well
Together such as brethren are in unity to dwell
It is an honour for men to cease from strife.

Canongate Tolbooth
031–225 2424 x 6638. Marked by an overlarge Victorian clock which sticks out over the pavement, the present building dates from 1591, when the tower and courtroom block were built on the site of an earlier 'tolbuith'. Quite picturesque, with its forestair and stair turret, it has variously served as courthouse, prison and municipal centre for the independent burgh of Canongate, and now houses a museum (temporary exhibitions and brass rubbing centre). The J. Telfer Dunbar Tartan Collection is kept here. *Open Oct–May 10.00–17.00 Mon–Sat; June–Sep 10.00–18.00 Mon–Sat and 14.00–17.00 on Suns during the Festival. Admission free.*

Canongate Church
Completed on the orders of James VII in 1691 after he ousted the congregation from the nave of Holyrood Abbey, which he converted to a chapel for the Order of the Thistle.

Standing back from the road in a churchyard rich with memorials, rounded gables rise above round arched windows and a slightly awkward Roman Doric portico. In the churchyard are memorials to many of Scotland's best loved sons – a fascinating place to explore. Look for the grave of Robert Fergusson, the poet who inspired Robert Burns. When Burns found his grave neglected and overgrown he paid for the stone you now see. There is also a bronze relief marked 'Clarinda'. Actually Mrs Agnes Maclehose, or Nancy, had been abandoned by her husband, who had gone to Jamaica. With two children to look after she was lonely, and formed a very close friendship with Robert Burns, and they exchanged letters continually – she 'Clarinda', he 'Sylvander'. It was of her that he wrote:
'Had we never lov'd sae kindly
Had we never lov'd sae blindly
Never met or never parted
We had ne'er been broken hearted.'
Burns died in 1796, she some years later, when his letters to her were found.

Dunbar's Close
A beautifully re-created formal 17thC garden enclosed by high walls and entered through iron gates. An ideal place

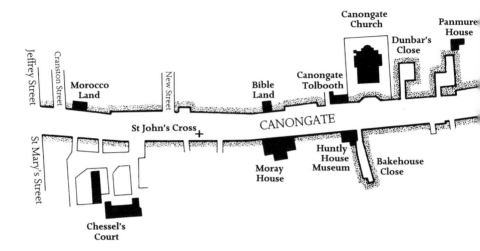

to rest when walking the Royal Mile. It was laid out in 1978.

Panmure House
Secreted in Panmure Close, this 17thC house with crow-stepped gables, by Adam Smith, was once the house of the Jacobite Earls of Panmure, and more notably Adam Smith from 1778 until his death in 1790. Philosopher and economist, he wrote *An Enquiry into the Nature and Causes of the Wealth of Nations* (1776).

White Horse Close
An extensively restored but wholly enjoyable recreation of the original 17thC buildings, less a forestair or two. The coach for London used to leave from the White Horse Inn, which once stood at the rear of the close. The horses were stabled below.

Abbey Strand
The three S's in the road are a reminder that debtors could find sanctuary in the 17thC tenements here. When imprisonment for debt ended in 1880, the need for sanctuary also ended.

South Side
Downhill towards Holyrood

Cannonball House
A cannon ball embedded in the stonework of the west wall gives the building its name. Whether it was a shot fired from the Castle during the Jacobite

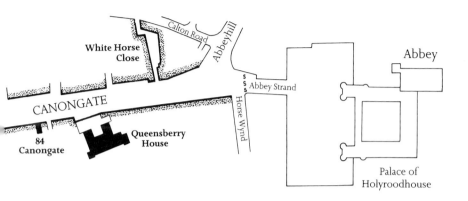

siege of 1745, or simply a marker indicating the gravitation height of the city's first water supply, is not known. It is known that the building dates from 1630 and was built onto an earlier structure for Alexander Mure. His initials, and those of his wife, can be seen above the small dormer on the west side. Remodelled in 1913, Cannonball House now serves as a handsome annexe to Castlehill School.

Boswell's Court
A large tenement built for Thomas Lowthian circa 1600, and not at all improved by its cement rendering. It has a fine moulded and inscribed doorway. The court is named after the uncle of James Boswell, biographer of Dr Johnson.

Tolbooth Church
Affectionately known as the Highland Church, this magnificently detailed Gothic Revival building was designed by James Gillespie Graham and A.W.N. Pugin 1839–44. Its octagonal spire, fully 74m tall, takes full advantage of its elevated position at the top of the Royal Mile. Intended to serve both as a local church and as a meeting hall for the General Assembly of the Church of Scotland, it has committee rooms on the ground floor with the church above. Inside it is light and airy, with a finely ribbed ceiling, but there is no access at time of writing, and this splendid building looks a little down at heel.

Riddle's Court
Situated in the inner court is the mansion of Bailie John McMorran, built in

1590 and one of the finest surviving examples of a wealthy merchant's house, with richly decorated interiors and a curious curved outside wooden stair. McMorran himself did not live here long, being shot in 1595 by a High School student during a riot over shortened school holidays. Such was the stature of the mansion, however, that it was used for a banquet given by the Town Council in honour of James VI and his Queen. It was restored in 1964 and is now an adult education centre. Riddle's Court was also the home of David Hume, philosopher and historian, when he first came to Edinburgh in 1751.

Brodie's Close
Initially evocative of the old Edinburgh, the illusion is eventually shattered when the close opens onto a totally unsympathetic new building. It is a great pity, for it takes its name from Francis Brodie, father of William Brodie, Deacon of Wrights and Masons – cabinet-maker by day, and burglar by night. Eventually recognised, he was hanged, along with his accomplice, on gallows of his own design on 1 October 1788. Three brass studs at the corner of George the IV Bridge mark this spot, which is also overlooked by the tavern bearing his name. Robert Louis Stevenson used Brodie as the inspiration from which he wove the tale of *Dr Jekyll and Mr Hyde.*

Heart of Midlothian
A brass plaque enclosed by a heart shaped arrangement of cobble stones marks the site of the Edinburgh Tolbooth, erected in the 14thC and finally pulled down in 1817. Used variously as the Scottish Parliament, a Court of Law and a jail, it was this last role that Sir Walter Scott immortalised in his work, *The Heart of Midlothian* (1818). Tradition has it that one should spit upon this spot

– thankfully modern etiquette frowns upon this practice.

St Giles' Cathedral
Strictly the High Kirk of the City of Edinburgh, since it was only a Cathedral in the true sense for the years 1633–8 and 1661–89, following the introduction of bishops to the Presbyterian Church of Scotland by Charles I. The title has stuck, perhaps because of its prominent position halfway along the High Street. There has been a church on this site since AD 854, although the present building is mainly medieval with some fragments of Norman work, all enclosed inside a Georgian exterior. The distinctive crowned tower, topped with a gold weather vane, dates from the late 15thC, and thankfully escaped the refacing of 1829–33 carried out by William Burn, who sought to simplify the structure and make it more cathedral-like. The result is not impressive, except perhaps in scale.

This restoration was prompted in part by the removal of the Old Tolbooth (at the Heart of Midlothian) and the Luckenbooths in 1817. The latter were a closely packed row of lock-up shops standing virtually against the wall of the cathedral, leaving only the narrowest of alleys between. This was the 'stink and style' mentioned by William Dunbar around 1500. It is worth examining an excellent miniature reconstruction of the Royal Mile in the Huntly House Museum in Canongate to gain an impression of how it all looked. The Thistle Chapel, with its impressively ornamented Gothic interior by Robert Lorimer, was added in 1909–11. The real delights of St Giles' are to be found inside, where much of the original medieval work can be seen. Indeed the choir has been noted as the finest piece of late medieval parish church architecture in Scotland.

Mercat Cross

The original was first mentioned in 1365 since when it has occupied five separate sites in the High Street, one of which is marked in the cobbles by the entrance to Old Fishmarket Close. The cross, as well as once being a drinking fountain, has served as an important focus of events in Scotland's turbulent past, for it was from here that Royal Proclamations, such as the dissolution of Parliament, are read three days after their announcement in London (or the time it took to complete the journey on horseback). The present cross incorporates part of the shaft of the 16thC one.

Charles II Statue

A unique life-sized statue depicting the King as Caesar, cast in lead and supplied by James Smith in 1685. It is thought to have come from Holland.

Parliament House and the Law Courts

031–225 2595. A complex array of buildings behind an uninspiring neo-classical facade designed by Robert Reid and built in 1808.

The supreme civil court, the Court of Session, was established in Edinburgh by James V in 1532. This also became the assembly place of the Scottish Parliament, which followed the court from the Old Tolbooth (where it was held until 1560, see Heart of Midlothian above) to the west end of St Giles' until Charles I ordered the building of Parliament Hall. Completed in 1639, it remained in use until the Union of 1707. Additional buildings were added to house the various court functions and advocates' libraries. It is now the home of the Scottish Law Courts.

Of particular note is the magnificent hammerbeam roof of the Parliament Hall (*Open 09.00–16.30 Tue–Fri. Closed Sat, Sun, Mon and public hols*), made of Danish oak by John Scott, Master Wright to the City of Edinburgh. On winter days a fine roaring open fire burns in one of the richly decorated fireplaces. The south window (which was being restored in 1987) depicts the founding of the College of Justice by James V. It was designed by Wilhelm von Kaulbach. There are statues of Viscount Melville, Robert Dundas, Lord Cockburn, Duncan Forbes, Lord Jeffrey, Lords President Boyle and Blair and Sir Walter Scott. And, of course, the whole place is alive with the usual subdued bustle of a court of law. The wonderfully light and airy Signet Library, which is not open to the

'Half Hangit Maggie'

Margaret Dickson was a much loved 18thC High Street fishwife, who became pregnant by a Kelso innkeeper's son after her husband deserted her. Born prematurely, the child died and Maggie's attempts to conceal the body resulted in her being found guilty under the Concealment of Pregnancy Act of 1690 and on 2 September 1724 she was hanged near St Giles. After a scuffle with some medical students who wanted her body for research, she was put in a coffin by her friends and taken by cart to be buried at Musselburgh. But in the graveyard Maggie started moaning, and when the lid was lifted, she was found to be alive. Perplexed magistrates had to agree that having been officially pronounced dead, she could not be sentenced again. She lived another 40 years, known to her friends and all as 'Half Hangit Maggie'.

public, has elegant Corinthian columns beneath a saucer dome roof by William Stark.

Borthwick's Close

A close which conjures up visions of old Edinburgh. Wander through its irregular arches, over uneven paving slabs hemmed in by high walls and you will see the building which was once George Heriot's Hospital School, built in 1839 in Jacobean style and currently being gutted and rebuilt.

New Assembly Close

An 18thC wing of the Commercial Bank building built by James Gillespie Graham in 1814 (see Wax Museum below) was used as Assembly Rooms between 1736 and 1784, the venue for many dancing assemblies, an 18thC passion. Later the masonic Lodge St David met here, attended by Sir Walter Scott. Between 1780–1812 it became the King's Arms Tavern.

Edinburgh Wax Museum

142 High St. 031–226 4445. Opened in the Commercial Bank Building in 1976 it contains a display of costumed models arranged in a series of tableaux illustrating aspects of Scottish history as well as other famous figures. There is also a special children's section and the inevitable chamber of horrors. Separate is the Visions of Tomorrow Gallery of Holography, a fascinating exhibition of 3D pictures produced with lasers. Some are for sale. *Open 10.00–17.00 Mon–Sun. Admission charge.*

The Tron Kirk

A finely proportioned and extremely handsome building, it takes its name from the public weighing beam, or tron, which once stood close by. It was built 1636–47 by John Mylne Jnr and John Scott to accommodate the congregation of St Giles' when the latter became a cathedral. Reconstructed 1785–7 by John Baxter Jnr, it was severely damaged in the great fire of 1824 and the original tower was subsequently demolished. Rebuilt to a taller classical design by R & R Dickson in 1828, a remarkably successful marriage of 17thC and 19thC styles was achieved.

Now again re-opened for exhibitions it is once again possible to inspect the stunning hammerbeam roof by John Scott, which is as fine a piece of work as that in Parliament Hall. The foundations have been excavated to reveal the layout of Marlin's Wynd, and the earliest examples of street paving in the city, laid in 1532. The Tron is the traditional assembly place on Hogmanay and, in spite of the distractions of television, a substantial and merry crowd still gathers to hear the pipes, and to sing the New Year in.

Museum of Childhood

031–225 2424 x 6646. Devoted to the history of childhood, this is an enchanting, colourful, noisy place. Dolls, trains, models, games, mechanical amusements and books crowd the displays. Adults will love it as much as the children. *Open Jun–Sep 10.00–18.00 Mon–Sat and 14.00–17.00 on Suns during the Festival. Oct–May 10.00–17.00 Mon–Sat. Admission free.*

Tweeddale Court

In 1806, when this was the headquarters of the British Linen Bank, William Begbie, a messenger, was robbed and murdered in the narrow entrance. Tweeddale House dates from the 16thC and was built by Neil Lang, Keeper of the Signet. Sir William Bruce bought it in 1664, and in turn sold it in 1670 to the second Earl of Tweeddale. It was subsequently altered and extended. The shed on the west side of the court is thought to have been used to garage sedan chairs – although this is impossible to confirm.

World's End Close

The first and last close when it was just inside the city wall.

Chessel's Court

The well restored block of mansion flats is Chessel's Buildings, erected in 1748 by Archibald Chessel for the well-to-do. Later used as the excise office, it was here that Deacon Brodie was caught stealing here in 1788 (see Brodie's Close, on page 38), and subsequently hanged.

St John's Cross

A cobbled cross in the road indicates the site of St John's Cross, which marked the boundary of land owned by the Order of St John. The Scottish headquarters of the Knights of St John is in St John Street nearby.

Moray House

Mary, Dowager Countess of Horne built this fine mansion around 1625, and passed it to her daughter Margaret, Countess of Moray (from whom it takes its name) in 1643. The earliest part of the building adjoins Canongate, which is overhung by a fine corbelled balcony. A gateway, guarded by two overlarge spikes, gives access to the gardens. Charles I was a frequent visitor, and Oliver Cromwell is known to have stayed here twice. There is a story that the Treaty of Union, which united the Parliaments of Scotland and England, was signed in the summer house here. Although quite possible, it cannot be confirmed (see also Queensberry House). Moray House is now used as a teacher training college, so unfortunately there is no public access to the richly decorated interior, which has some excellent moulded ceilings. You might be able to see some of these from the road, if the interior lights are on.

Huntly House Museum

031-225 2424 x 6689. This was never a great town house, as the name implies, but an amalgamation of three houses built into one in 1570. Bought in 1647 by the Incorporation of Hammermen, and used as a meeting house, they employed Robert Mylne to enlarge the frontage and convert it into flats. This work was completed in 1671. It takes its name from George, first Marquess of Huntly, who had lodgings here in 1636. After the building of the New Town, Huntly House degenerated into a slum along with most of the other buildings in Canongate. Shops were built into the ground floor – one of which, at the turn of this century, was called the Poet's Box. Here you could buy popular contemporary sheet music. One such ditty was meaningfully entitled *Never Push a Man Because He's Going Down the Hill*.

Its humble beginnings should certainly not discourage a visit, however, for the wealth of original fittings, panelling and fireplaces to be seen is quite staggering. The restoration was executed by Frank C. Mears in 1927–32, who replicated the inscribed Latin panels which gave rise to the building's 19thC nick-name, the Speaking House. Rambling through passageways, and in rooms of differing levels, the exhibits and period room settings give a great insight into the past life of Edinburgh. There are important collections of local silver, glass and pottery, and, of particular interest to those exploring the Royal Mile, an excellent miniature reconstruction of how it would have appeared in the 17thC and 18thC. *Open Jun–Sep 10.00–18.00 Mon–Sat and 14.00–17.00 on Suns during the Festival. Oct–May 10.00–17.00 Mon–Sat. Admission free.*

Bakehouse Close

Entered through a broad arch beneath Huntly House, Bakehouse Close offers a very handsome glimpse of old Edinburgh. At its head is **Acheson House**, built in 1633 by Secretary of State Sir Archibald Acheson and restored in 1937. The main entrance is now from Canongate, and the building houses the Scottish Craft Centre. Note the inscription above the entrance to the north courtyard: *O Lord in thee is al my traist* (O Lord in thee is all my trust), and the monogram and crest above the stair tower door.

84 Canongate

A 1953 replica front of Nisbet of Dirleton's house, which has re-used a very fine inscribed lintel and stones dated 1619.

Queensberry House

Lord Halton began building this great mansion in 1681, with James Smith as his mason, and sold the completed work to the first Duke of Queensberry in 1686. Used variously as flats, a barracks, people's refuge and now as a hospital for the elderly, it is best known as the home of the second Duke of Queensberry.

A staunch supporter of the Treaty of Union, the Duke is reported to have accepted a bribe of £12,325 to ensure its signing. This did little to make him popular with the Edinburgh folk, who spread the story that his son, known to be insane, was caught eating a kitchen boy whom he had just spit-roasted.

The Palace of Holyroodhouse

What is now a palace probably originated as the guest house of the Abbey of Holyrood. The Abbey was founded by David I in 1128 on the spot, where legend has it, he was saved from an enraged stag by divine intervention. William Harrison (1534–93) described the events in his translation of *The Description of Scotland*, first written in Latin by Hector Boethius:

'He was admonished in his sleepe, that he should build an abbeie for a religious order to live in together. Where upon he sent for workmen into France and Flanders, and set them in hand to build this abbeie of canons regular, as he was admonished, dedicating it in honor of a crosse for that verie strangelie it slipped into his hands as he was pursuing and following of a hart in the chase'.

Being a royal foundation conferred upon it great status, and it is likely that from the earliest times the accommodation had been designed as suitable for a king. In 1174 the bishops and nobles of Scotland met at Holyrood to discuss raising a ransom for William the Lion, captured at Alnwick while trying to recover Northumberland. Later, in 1177, the Pope's envoy, Vivian, held council there. During the period 1195–1230 the church was rebuilt on a much grander scale and by 1329 it seems certain that it was used as a royal residence. With the burial in the choir of David II in 1370 the royal connection was irreversibly made. Indeed royal interments continued until 1566, when Henry Lord Darnley, husband of Mary Queen of Scots strangled at Kirk o'Field, was buried here.

James II, born at Holyrood in 1426, was crowned there six years later, married there in 1449 and was finally buried there in 1460 after being killed by an exploding cannon during the siege of Roxburgh Castle, near Kelso.

James IV embarked on an extensive re-building programme 1501–5 in preparation for his marriage to Margaret Tudor in 1508, which included the construction of a new south tower, and royal apartments, giving the Palace the basic form which survives today. His son, James V continued the reconstruction, but it all came to a sorry end in 1544 when the Earl of Hertford sacked Edinburgh. The abbey was desecrated further during the Reformation although the nave of the church was still used as the parish church of Canongate, the choir and transepts being demolished in 1570.

Holyrood, in history and romance, is strongly associated with Mary Queen of Scots. She lived at Holyrood from 1564–70 during the traumatic years of her husband, Lord Darnley's death and the murder of

David Rizzio, her secretary.

Improvement to the fabric of Holyrood continued, with major works being undertaken prior to the coronation of Charles I in 1633; yet again it was damaged by fire, this time whilst occupied by Cromwell's troops in 1650.

With the re–establishment of the monarchy in 1660 came the restoration of Holyrood Palace. The Scottish Parliament and Privy Council voted a large sum for rebuilding in the new Palladian style, retaining only the North West Tower. Designs were prepared by Sir William Bruce of Balcaskie, and Robert Mylne, Charles II's Master Mason, was employed to execute the work. Finally completed in 1679, the result was sumptuous. The finest quarried stone from Fife and South Queensferry, Dutch tiles, Italian marble and English and French glass were all used to great effect. It is largely this rebuilt Palace one sees today. James Duke of York and Duchess Mary of Modena immediately took up residence, to escape religious agitation in England. The new Council Chamber was converted into a Roman Catholic chapel in 1686 on the orders of James VII, who also used the abbey church for the revived Order of the Thistle – none of which impressed the Protestants who frenziedly destroyed all his work.

Following the Act of Union in 1707 the Palace was transformed into an exclusive lodging house for the nobles, and the Great Apartment built by Charles II was left abandoned. The ground in front of the Palace became a debtor's sanctuary, the boundary of which is still marked by a series of S's in the road.

Royal patronage returned in the shape of Charles Edward Stuart, the Young Pretender, and his entourage during the abortive rebellion of 1745, although he did not occupy the Great Apartment, preferring to stay in the Duke of Hamilton's apartment in the North West Tower, using the Gallery for his receptions.

The final refurbishment of Holyroodhouse, and its reinstatement as a Royal Palace, was ordered by George IV during his visit to Scotland in 1822. Robert Reid supervised the work, which was completed by 1834. A new courthouse and gaol were built for the Bailie of Holyrood Abbey (for the debtors within the sanctuary), as was a new stable block. Queen Victoria stayed at the Palace of Holyroodhouse during her visit to Scotland in 1842, and the last of the nobles was finally evicted in 1852. Two years later part of the buildings were opened to the public, and in 1871 a private suite of rooms for the use of the monarch were prepared. During this century, the Palace is the Royal Family's official Scottish home and is constantly used by them when visiting Scotland. The Lord High Commissioner also lives there during the annual General Assembly of the Church of Scotland.

The Abbey, since the coronation of Charles I in 1633, has suffered from neglect and ineptitude. Its use as the Canongate parish church ended in 1687, and its fittings were destroyed in the revolution of the following year when the mob overpowered the 100-strong guard and reduced the place to an unsightly heap of ruins. This completed, they marched in procession to the Mercat Cross, with bands playing, and there burnt an effigy of the Pope. A roof of stone slabs laid over the high vault in 1758 collapsed 10 years later, causing considerable damage. Twentieth century restoration schemes were rejected. The shell of the abbey was to remain much as we see it today. *Open for guided tours only 09.30–15.15 Mon–Sat, 10.30–16.30 Sun; Nov–Mar 09.30–15.45. Closed Sun. Also closed during royal and state visits. Tours last 35 mins and start every 10–15 mins in the summer high season. Admission charge.*

Palace Yard Gates

Built in 1922 as a memorial to Edward VII, they were designed by Sir George Washington Browne, and feature the Lion and the Unicorn overlooking some very fine ironwork.

Holyrood Park

An oasis of peace not far from the busy city centre. See chapter on Parks, Gardens and Viewpoints.

The Fountain

The over ornamented fountain was designed by Robert Matheson and dates from 1859. It was apparently inspired by the Cross Well at Linlithgow, built in 1628.

Sun Dial

In the garden to the north west of the James IV tower. It has carvings of various heraldic badges and the crowned initials of Charles I. **Queen Mary's Bath House** stands in a corner of the one time garden. She was reputed to have bathed here in wine.

The Palace Interiors

(Areas described are those usually open to the public)

The State Staircase

The broad stairway has a stone balustrade, with walls embellished with displays of broadswords, tapestries and paintings. The fine plasterwork of the ceiling depicting the Honours of Scotland dates from 1678–9 and is by John Houlbert. In the corners, angels blow trumpets.

The Throne Room

This was originally the Guard Hall, and is one of the suite of three rooms (the Evening and Morning Drawing Rooms are the other two) used for ceremonials and receptions. The panelling and ceiling is a copy of 17thC work; the fireplace survives from the redecoration of 1856.

Evening Drawing Room

The oak panelling is modern, the ceiling, by John Houlbert, dates from 1676.

The Palace of Holyroodhouse

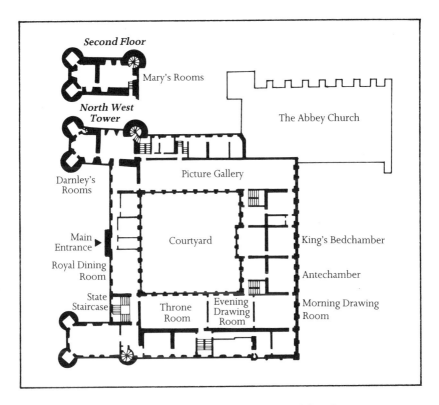

Morning Drawing Room

This was once the Privy Chamber, and is lavishly decorated. The overmantle and doorcases have fine woodwork by Alexander Eizat (1677) and paintings by Jacob de Witt. The ceiling again is by Houlbert (1676), plasterwork of cherubs holding the Honours of Scotland, with the monogram CR in wreaths, and unicorns above the fireplace. The panelling is modern, but the furniture is mainly 18thC. A stool, embroidered by Queen Mary, wife of King George V, can be seen here.

Antechamber

Early panelling in here also by Eizat, dating from 1677. The painting in the overmantle is by Jacob de Witt.

The King's Bedchamber

The most sumptuously decorated and furnished room in the Great Apartment, the visible manifestation of the wealth and influence of the monarch, Charles II. The ceiling, heavily decorated with foliage and royal emblems, is by Houlbert and Dunsterfield, enclosing an oval painting by de Witt circa 1677. The chimney piece, carved with lion heads, is by Jan van Santvoort. The panelling and massive state bed date from the 17thC, and many of the other pieces of furniture were made specially for the Palace. Leading on from the King's Bedroom is the closet, similarly decorated.

The Picture Gallery

Occupying the whole of the north

47

range, 47m long and 7m wide, and created in 1671 for Charles II who wished for a connection between his old apartment in the North West Tower and the grand new apartment in the east. It incorporates the north wall of the 16thC Palace, which may also have been part of the medieval abbey guesthouse. On the wood panelled walls hang the portraits of 80 real, and not so real, kings of Scotland, from Fergus I (circa 330 BC) to James VII. They were all painted by a hack painter, Jacob de Witt, who took two years to complete the lot, finishing in 1686 and receiving £120 for his trouble. The ceiling is very recent, although it uses 17thC motifs. The Gallery is used annually for a function given by the Lord High Commissioner to the General Assembly of the Church of Scotland. The south end of the Gallery opens into the lobby; in the 16thC this was the King's Wardrobe, later re-fitted as the Queen's Privy Chamber and now known as the Duchess of Hamilton's Room. The decorated ceiling by James Baine dates from 1672, and carries the monogram of Charles II.

Darnley's Rooms

Otherwise known as the Queen's Antechamber and Bedchamber, and located on the first floor of the North West Tower, they were occupied by Henry Lord Darnley, husband of Mary Queen of Scots 1564–7. The decoration, ceiling and panelling are all 17thC, as is the bed. The Antechamber is hung with tapestries. A narrow stair connects with Mary's rooms above.

Mary's Rooms

It was in the Audience Chamber that Mary interviewed John Knox, who implored her 'purge your heart from Papistry, and preserve you from the council of flatterers; for how pleasant they appear to your ear . . . experience hath taught us into what perplexity they have brought famous Princes'.

Of particular interest is the wooden ceiling, divided into 16 panels and decorated with motifs which recall 'the auld alliance' between Scotland and France. In the centre are the arms of Mary of Guise, Mary's mother. The ceiling dates from 1532. A painting, circa 1560, depicts the dead Lord Darnley, with his family praying for vengeance.

The inner chamber also has a fine 16thC wood panelled ceiling, which, like that in the Audience Chamber, survived the fire of 1650. A plaque in an outer room of the Queen's Chambers marks the spot where Rizzio, Mary's secretary, was stabbed to death.

The Royal Dining Room

Refurbished in Adam style in the late 18thC, as the Duke of Hamilton's Music Room, it overlooks the forecourt.

The Abbey Church

Built circa 1195 to 1230, it contains much original work in spite of the rebuilding prior to Charles I's coronation in 1633. However, continuous neglect and ineptitude since then have left it the roofless ruin we see today. Even the symmetry of its grand west front has been completely destroyed by the incursion of the Palace.

The New Town

Edinburgh is one of the most handsome cities in Europe and the New Town has some of its finest buildings. The capital expanded at a period of high taste in building; consequently the New Town is a beautiful example of commodious Georgian architecture. It is spacious, gracious and ordered. A wander through the shops and restaurants of Stockbridge, a shopping spree along Princes Street and a visit to the monuments on Calton Hill should all be on your agenda.

The first New Town was conceived to alleviate the hopeless, warren-like overcrowding of the Old. With 50,000 people living on 138 acres enclosed by the city wall it's no wonder disease and crime had become endemic. The city wall was built during the panic after Scotland's defeat by the English at Flodden in 1513. George Drummond, Lord Provost from 1725 to his death in 1766 was the main instigator of the first New Town. He is quoted in conversation with the Reverend Thomas Somerville, who recalled:

'I happened one day to be standing at a window looking out to the opposite side of the Nor' Loch (now Princes Street Gardens), then called Bearford's Parks, in which there was not a single house to be seen. "Look at these fields", said Provost Drummond, 'you Mr Somerville are a young man and may probably live, though I will not, to see all these fields covered with houses, forming a splendid and magnificent city. To the accomplishment of this nothing more is necessary than draining the Nor' Loch and providing a proper access from the Old Town.'

Bearford's Parks had in fact been purchased by the City in 1716, but it was not until 1752 that Drummond's 'Proposals' were published, and subsequently given weight by an Act of Parliament the following year. By 1759 more land had been purchased, and the huge project of draining the Nor' Loch began. Drummond laid the foundation stone of the North Bridge in 1763. This was followed by the acquisition of further land – much of it purchased privately by city officials, speculating on the vast profits to be made when the building began – until an advertisement was published, in March 1766, for the submission of plans. Drummond died later that year, giving substance to his prophesy that he would not see the realisation of his dream.

A total of six schemes were submitted, and on 2 August 1766 the new Lord Provost and John Adam decided to accept the proposals of James Craig, an unknown 23-year-old architect, son of an Edinburgh merchant. His reward was immediate fame, a gold medal and the freedom of the city. Amended in consultation with John Adam, Lord

Kaimes and other notables of Edinburgh, his scheme was formally adopted in July 1767.

James Craig's plan, a regular grid-iron layout of broad streets, squares and gardens was simple yet ingenious, and took full advantage of the site. George Street which forms the broad central axis, 30m wide, straddles a natural ridge with spectacular views to the north and south. The east and west boundaries are defined by Charlotte and St Andrew Squares. Along the outer edges of the rectangular site were Queen Street and Princes Street, 24m wide, built up along one side only and overlooking gardens. Between these grand streets, intended for the rich and prosperous, were the narrower Thistle Street and Rose Street, where the respectable middle classes could build. Cutting across the long axis and linking the whole were Charlotte, Castle, Frederick, Hanover and St David Streets, all 24m wide. It is apparent from the names chosen for these streets that the Act of Union of 1707 was still fresh in everyone's mind, and that this exciting new scheme should symbolise it. St Andrew and St George (later to become Charlotte after Queen Charlotte) the respective patron saints of Scotland and England, Thistle Street and Rose Street, the two national emblems, Princes, Queen and Frederick (George's son) were all to be glorified.

Despite Craig's bold and imaginative design, building began reluctantly, and it was soon realised that incentives would have to be offered to start the ball rolling. John Young was given £20 when he built the first house in the New Town, in Thistle Street, off St Andrew Square. John Neale built the first house in Princes Street in 1769, earning for himself an exemption from rates. Gradually sites were taken up and the development began to take shape in a rather hotchpotch fashion. For although Craig had designed the street plan, there had been no specifications drawn up for the buildings which were to line them. In 1782 the city devised a set of rules which were to give the main streets some uniformity whilst still allowing for individual expression within the constraints imposed: each house was to be of three storeys plus basement, and to have a maximum width of just over 14m. Failure to comply was met with a fine and demolition.

Competition grew amongst architects to design here, and as terraces and larger public buildings appeared, the first New Town became a coherent whole.

Robert and John Adam, Sir William Chambers and John Henderson, the premier architects of the age, all contributed and in so doing inspired others. How pleased Provost Drummond would have been had he been able to see it. The first New Town is a superb, self-contained development which has retained its integrity in spite of the replacement of many of the original buildings with lesser Victorian and 20thC structures. Informed opinion suggests Craig drew his inspiration from the layout of Inverary in Argyll. He had, after all, been advised by John Adam and it was he, and his father, who had planned Inverary in 1747. The potential of one sided streets had already been fully exploited in Bath, and Edinburgh was another perfect site for the use of this idea.

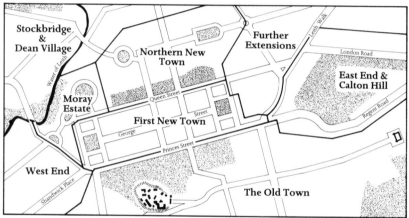

The Development of the New Town

New Town Conservation Centre
13a Dundas St. 031–556 7054. Display of conservation work, library and exhibition. Guided tours. *Open 09.00–13.00, 14.00–17.00 Mon–Fri. Admission free.*

First New Town Buildings

Charlotte Square and the
Georgian House   B3
If you have neither the time nor the inclination to see more of the New Town (and that would be a pity, for there is plenty to enjoy), then this is the one place you should under no cir-

cumstances miss. Robert Adam's masterpiece of urban architecture on the north side is, perhaps, more than any other, the essence of the New Town.

The National Trust for Scotland has had its headquarters in number 5 since 1949. They have owned numbers 5, 6 and 7 since 1966 when they fell into the hands of the Commissioners of Inland Revenue in part payment of estate duty, following the death of the 5th Marquess of Bute. The 4th Marquess had restored the buildings to their original appearance during the 1920s. Number 6 now serves as the official residence of the Secretary of State for Scotland, and number 7 is the renowned Georgian House.

The Georgian House

Furnished in 1974–5 as a typical example of the house of a wealthy family during the reign of George III. The entrance hall has a stone flagged floor, and leads to an inner hall and dining room, with a reeded black marble Adam fireplace. To the rear is a bedroom with a fireplace from Tarvit House, Fife. The basement kitchen is particularly fascinating, being equipped with a full range of period implements. On the first floor are the drawing room and library, the former having an exceptionally fine carved fireplace taken from number 5. The top of the house is private, being the residence of the Moderator of the General Assembly of the Church of Scotland.

Number 7 was built by Edward Butterworth, who speculated on several houses in the New Town. It was first sold to John Lamont of Lamont, later to be occupied by the Farquharson family of Invercauld from 1816–45, and subsequently until 1889 by Lord Neaves, a member of the Scottish bar. 031–226 5922. National Trust Shop. *Open May–Oct 10.00–17.00 Mon–Sat, 14.00–17.00 Sun. Nov 10.00–16.30 Sat, 14.00–16.30 Sun. Closed Dec–Mar. Admission charge.*

Robert Adam designed this north block in 1791, and it was completed following his death in 1792 by Robert Reid. Each house typically comprised a parlour, library and dining room on the ground floor, a drawing room and bedrooms on the first floor, more bedrooms on the second floor, with smaller bedrooms in the attic. A kitchen, store room and utility room took up the basement, giving a total of some 18 rooms to be occupied by a family of three to eight persons supported by as many as nine servants. Curiously there are no attendant buildings – coach houses or stables – which would have been expected for a house of this status.

Number 6, although not open to the public, has particularly splendid interiors and an interesting history of occupancy. Built in 1797 by Orlando Hart, an Edinburgh shoemaker, it was the home of Sir John Sinclair of Ulbster from 1806–16. His portrait, by Raeburn, can be seen in the National Gallery of Scotland, wearing the uniform of the Caithness Fencibles. It was Sinclair who initiated the mammoth Statistical Account of Scotland, intended as a basis for social planning. Later, between 1825–44, the house was used as a hotel by Charles Oman, which eventually extended into number 4.

Number 5, the National Trust's headquarters, was built in 1796 by Adam and Charles Russell, who sold it to John Grant of Rothiemurchus, Grant's daughter, Elisabeth, who wrote *Memoirs of a Highland Lady* was born here in 1797. The whole north block can, and should, be admired from across Charlotte Square, the visible manifestation of the lifestyle of the monied and leisured classes of 18thC Edinburgh.

The following section is a selection of the most notable buildings and monuments within the area of the first New Town, grouped under the various street names. Of course many of the original buildings have now disappeared, so some later replacements are included.

Princes Street
Edinburgh's main shopping street.

St John's Episcopal Church   B4
West end of Princes St. A handsome revived perpendicular building, built 1815–18 by William Burn. The tall, spacious, arcaded interior is a masterly piece of work.

St Cuthbert's Parish Church   C4
Entrance in Lothian Rd. There is no trace now of the medieval building, the present church (by Hippolyte Blanc) dates from 1895 but incorporates an 18thC steeple. Its situation is remarkably picturesque, but its furnishings are extraordinary. John Napier, inventor of logarithms, is buried in the graveyard.

The Mound   E4
This came into being when building in the New Town was at its height. Over 1800 cartloads of mud and rubble from the excavations were dumped here each day with the final total calculated at 1,305,780 loads. Begun by George Boyd, a Lawnmarket clothier, in 1781, it soon became a convenient short cut between the Old and New Towns, known as 'Geordie Boyd's Mud Brig'. Excavations were also used to fill the drained Nor' Loch, which then became private gardens for the Princes Street residents. When the Mound was opened as a thoroughfare, buildings in the Lawnmarket were pulled down to clear the way. Among them was George Boyd's shop. The Mound was one of the first paved areas to be fitted with an electric road blanket in 1959, to prevent snow lying.

Royal Scottish Academy   E3
The Mound. An austere Doric temple by William Playfair built 1822–6 and altered by him in 1831–6. Inside hang the works of academicians and invited artists.

National Gallery   E4
The Mound. Also by Playfair in the same classic style, but rather awkwardly juxtaposed with the Royal Scottish Academy due to the road alignment. See also Galleries and Museums (page 138).

Scott Monument   E3
031–225 2424 x 6596. An elaborate buttressed Gothic steeple rising some 61m above Princes Street, beneath which sits Sir Walter Scott with Maida, his faithful deerhound, at his side. The whole statue is carved from a 30 ton chunk of Carrara marble by John Steell 1840–6. A subscription was raised after Scott's death in 1832 and in 1836 a competition was launched to design a suitable memorial. The winning design was that submitted by George Meikle Kemp, carpenter son of a border shepherd and a self-taught architect. Regrettably he did not live to appreciate his work, being found drowned in the Union Canal two years before the monument was finally completed in 1846. The builder, David Lind, sunk foundations 16m deep to rest on solid rock and the total cost, including the statue, was £15,000, a stark contrast with the £154,000 spent on restoration in the mid-1970s. Sixty-four characters from Scott's novels and poetry decorate the tower. The panoramic view from the uppermost gallery, is well worth the long climb up the 287 steps. Open Nov–Feb 09.00–18.00 Mon–Sat; Oct–Mar 09.00–15.00 Mon–Sat. Admission charge.

Jenners   E3
Princes St, on the corner of St David St. One of the largest department stores in Britain when it was built in 1893–5, and still an extremely endearing Renaissance building in warm pink stone. Before you enter, look up at the elaborate detailing, the carved figures and bold octagonal corner turret. Inside, spare a moment to enjoy the gallery.

George Street
The headquarters of Scotland's financial institutions are located in George Street.

Royal Bank of Scotland   E3
14 George St. A grand porticoed building built in 1847 by David Rhind on the site of James Craig's Physician's Hall (1775). The pedimental sculpture, carved in high relief by A. Handyside Ritchie, is of particular note.

George IV Statue   D3
Where George St meets Hanover St. In bronze by Francis Chantrey, it commemorates George IV's visit to Edinburgh in 1822.

Church of St Andrew and St George   C3
West end of George St. An unusual oval building fronted by a portico supported on columns which stand virtually at pavement level. The tall steeple, 51m high rises in four stages and is particularly handsome. The Church was designed by Major Andrew Frazer of the Royal Engineers in 1782–4. Appointed Scottish Engineer-in-Chief in 1779, this is thought to be his only building. Dr Welsh, Professor of Church History in the University of Edinburgh, led the great 'Disruption' of 1843 from here. He left the meeting of the General Assembly with 193 ministers, to be joined outside by a further 300 supporters, who marched down Hanover Street to an alternative venue at Canonmills, and established the Free Church of Scotland.

Bank of Scotland   D3
101–3 George St. A beautifully proportioned and finely detailed building by J.M. Dick Peddic, built 1883–5. The contrasting treatment of the two doorways is interesting – had they both been porticoed, much of the building's charm would have been lost.

Queen Street
Queen Street remains the least altered of the First New Town streets, where sequences of 18thC houses can still be seen.

Royal College of Physicians   C2
9 Queen St. A restrained Neo-Classical frontage adorned with statues by A. Handyside Ritchie. Designed by Thomas Hamilton in 1844, it replaced an earlier house. Note the superb cast iron lamps, modelled with gilded cocks.

Scottish National Portrait Gallery   E2
Eastern end of Queen St. Built 1885–90 as a gift to the nation from J.R. Findlay, owner of The Scotsman newspaper. Architecturally it is both interesting yet disappointing – the blank upper wall (to accommodate the galleries inside) being particularly conspicuous. The sculptures in the niches between the windows at first floor level, by W. Birnie Rhind are, however, a redeeming feature (see also page 138).

St Andrew Square
The many financial and insurance offices make this the city's wealthiest area, along with George Street.

The Melville Monument   E2
Centrepiece of St Andrew Square, erected 1820–3. The column is 41m high and was intended to rival the Trajan column in Rome. The figure of Henry Dundas (Lord Melville), Pitt's Navy Treasurer and a very influential man of his time, stands statuesquely on its top.

Royal Bank of Scotland   E2
St Andrew Sq. A very handsome and imposing house built in 1771 by William Chambers for Sir Laurence Dundas. The gilt Royal Arms was added by the Excise Office, who occupied the building from 1794; they also constructed the two-

storey wing. It was bought by the Royal Bank of Scotland in 1825 and was for a considerable time their head office. The interior is lit by a beautiful domed ceiling decorated with original and flamboyant star-shaped windows.

26 St Andrew Square   E2
An early (1770) rubble walled house designed by William Chambers, with a porch added in 1840. The adjoining buildings are original, but much altered.

39 St Andrew Square   F2
Initially built in 1846 by David Bryce for the British Linen Bank, it is now part of the Bank of Scotland. Above the ground floor six bold Corinthian pillars divide the richly detailed frontage into five bays. Standing proudly on top of the columns at roof level are six fine statues by A. Handyside Ritchie. They represent Navigation, Commerce, Manufacture, Science, Art and Agriculture. The telling hall is equally imposing.

Thistle Street   E2
1–2 Thistle Court, St Andrew Sq end. Probably the earliest surviving New Town architecture – a handsome pair of rubble-built houses dating from 1768.

Northern New Town

This development was planned by the Heriot Trust in 1801, on a fine sloping site overlooking the Firth of Forth and with views of distant Fife. It was built in response to the success of the first New Town, which was, by that time, well established as the fashionable place to live. Primarily residential in character, it represents the single most unified building scheme in Edinburgh, and survives largely unaltered today.

Craig's grid pattern of wide streets ('draughty parallelograms', as Robert

Louis Stevenson called them) was followed. Robert Reid, Master of the King's Works in Scotland, and William Sibbald, Superintendent of Works in the City oversaw the initial stages of the work, which was completed by Thomas Bonner and Thomas Brown. William Playfair (1789–1857), one of Edinburgh's most brilliant and prolific architects, made an outstanding contribution with the design of Royal Circus.

It is perhaps hard to imagine that there was serious opposition to the speculative nature of much of the building, and the despoiling of open farm land with streets and buildings. Clearly, not just a 20thC phenomenon. These feelings were eloquently expressed by Lord Cockburn in *Memorials of His Time* (1856):

'It was about this time that the Earl of Moray's ground to the north of Charlotte Square began to be broken up for being built on. . . . It was the beginning of a sad change, as we then felt. That well kept and almost evergreen field was the most beautiful piece of ground in immediate connection with the town, and led the eye agreeably over to our distant northern scenery. It would be some consolation if the buildings were worthy of the situation . . .'

Northern New Town Buildings
All excellent examples of late Georgian terraces, with fine views over the Forth.

Heriot Row
Begun in 1802 and designed by Reid and Sibbald. Number 17 was the boyhood home of Robert Louis Stevenson.

Royal Circus   C1
Completed in 1823 to the design of William H. Playfair, who built opposing crescents on the curving, falling road to Stockbridge, and managed to maintain

outstanding elegance and symmetry. It makes for a superb introduction to the streets behind.

St Mary's Church

Bellevue Crescent. The focal point of the crescent, its tall steeple topped by a slim dome and lantern towering high above the terraces either side. A Corinthian portico sits firmly on six columns, with steps raising the entrance well above pavement level. Designed by Thomas Brown, City Superintendent of Works, it was built in 1824.

Calton Hill and the East

Calton Hill is covered with a piecemeal, but fascinating, array of monuments; mostly designed by William H. Playfair, they dominate the city skyline to the east. Varying from the dignified to the eccentric.

The National Monument   H2

Begun as a memorial to the dead of the Napoleonic wars, it was never completed, due to lack of funds. Now a monument to over-enthusiasm, the foundation stone was laid, amidst great ceremony, in 1822, before the money required for the project had been raised. Twelve columns were built, at a cost of £1000 each, before it all came to a halt. Often referred to as Edinburgh's Folly, or Scotland's Pride and Poverty, this pseudo-Parthenon was designed by C.R. Cockerell and William H. Playfair. If completed, it would have been a church. Today it just adds credence to Edinburgh's claim to be the 'Athens of the north'.

Nelson Monument   H2

Calton Hill. 031–556 2716. A rather ungainly castellated tower built in five stages and resembling, either by chance or design, an upturned telescope. On top, some 30m high, is a mast with cross trees and a time ball, which drops at 12 noon GMT (13.00 during British summer time). It was originally intended as a visual signal to ships in the Forth. Now it is electronically controlled like the one o'clock gun. Designed by Robert Burn in 1807, the base of this Gothic tower was subsequently enclosed by a pentagonal building by Thomas Bonnar. It was 'originally intended to give accommodation to a few disabled seamen' but later 'leased to a vendor of soups and sweetmeats' to give 'visitors . . . the opportunity of . . . drinking to the memory of the great hero they commemorate'. There is access to the tower (note the carving of the San Josef over the entrance) although the rooms are now a private residence. There are 146 steps to the top, and the view over the city and the Forth is superb. *Open Nov–Feb 10.00–18.00 Tue–Sat, 13.00–18.00 Mon. Oct–Mar 10.00–15.00 Mon–Sat. Admission charge.*

City Observatory   H2

Calton Hill. Built in 1818 by William H. Playfair for his uncle, Professor John Playfair, president of the Astronomical Institution, the building takes the form of a cross with four Roman Doric porticos at the compass points, topped by a dome housing the telescope. This is mounted on a masonry pillar which protrudes up through the upper floor. The building also contains a transit instrument and an astronomical clock. At the south east corner of the perimeter wall is Playfair's monument to his uncle, built 1825–6. At the south west corner is the bold and handsome rubble walled Observatory House built into the living rock. Begun in 1776 by Thomas Short, an optician astronomer, it was finally completed by James Craig in 1792. Intended as an observatory, it was never properly furnished with instruments. Smoke from the railway forced the removal of the observatory to Blackford

Hill and the buildings were bought by the City. Shortly after, in 1895, the City dome was built at the north east corner. Not open to the public.

Dugald Stewart's Monument   H2
Calton Hill. Stewart was Professor of Moral Philosophy at the University, succeeding Adam Ferguson in 1830. Modelled on the monument of Lysicrates in Athens, there are no prizes for guessing it was designed by Playfair.

Old Calton Burying Ground   G3
Some very fine early headstones and memorials below the Governor's House of the Old Calton Jail (now demolished), the best of which is that to the philosopher David Hume, a cylindrical Roman design by Robert Adam (1777).

New Calton Burying Ground   J3
The remains were disturbed when Waterloo Place was cut through the Old Burying Ground and they were re-interred here. All is overlooked by a circular watch tower. Some early monuments were also transferred here.

Burns Monument   J3
By the New Burying Ground. An elaborate circular Greek temple by Thomas Hamilton, 1830, based on the Choragic Monument of Lysicrates in Athens. There is a chamber in the base which once contained relics of the great poet, and a statue by Flaxman. These can now be seen in Lady Stair's House.

Royal High School   H3
In a dominant position on the south face of Calton Hill, a sloping site requiring vast underbuilding. After much discussion and many changes of plan Thomas Hamilton was employed by the City to build this large school on a central site. Completed in 1829 his

design is that of a Greek temple flanked by colonnades and enclosed by two lesser temples facing slightly outwards at a lower level. Internal alterations were begun in 1978 to provide a chamber and rooms for the Scottish Assembly, which failed to materialise due to a lack of support during the 1978 referendum on devolution. Hamilton's building would have suited this function admirably.

The Moray Estate
The Earl of Moray advertised this 13 acre site for development in 1822. Bounded on one side by the Water of Leith, it was an odd shape, but one which William Burn took full advantage of, writing to the Earl in April 1822: 'I have been most anxious to produce (a design) totally different from the monotony of our present streets and squares'. His accompanying drawings were passed to architect, James Gillespie Graham, who produced the final design by July of that same year. It remains almost as it was originally conceived, and is well worth an evening stroll.

Western New Town

A prosperous area of late Georgian terraces and villas, where building continued into the early 20thC, and enlivened by the three spires of St Mary's Cathedral.

St Mary's Cathedral
Palmerston Place. The largest ecclesiastic building in Scotland built since the Reformation, and a massively self confident example of early Victorian Gothic architecture by G. Gilbert Scott 1874–1917. The central spire is 90m tall, and dominates the surrounding level ground. The West Doorway, flanked by two lesser spires, is richly decorated, with the scale of the building emphasised

by its proximity to Palmerston Place. The interior, although tending to be a little gloomy, is impressive, and some of the furnishings are worth a look.

The Cathedral was built as the result of a bequest by the Walker sisters, heirs of Sir Patrick Walker, who had made a fortune by letting their lands of Easter Coates during the building of the New Town. This, and their manor house, were given to the Episcopalian Church on condition that a Cathedral was built. The two western towers are named Barbara and Mary in their memory.

Stockbridge

An intriguing area of shops and restaurants, Stockbridge has maintained its own village identity within the city. Although the Georgian development continued here, it is generally less imposing. Note especially **Ann Street**, by James Milne, which has an almost rural feel thanks to its elevated site and the long front gardens. It is said this is attributable to the artist Henry Raeburn. As far as anyone knows, it is the only entire street in the world to be given to a woman as a birthday present. Raeburn was devoted to his wife and prepared the street for her as a surprise. On her birthday he gave it to his wife and named it Ann Street after her.

One hundred metres to the south is St Bernards well-house, by the Water of Leith, built in 1789 by Alexander Nasmyth for Lord Gardenstone, who claimed to have benefited from this mineral spring. This circular Roman temple replaced an earlier well-house, built in 1760.

Where Henderson Row meets Hamilton Place is the district of Silvermills. Traces of the mills remain on both sides of West Silvermills Lane.

Dean Village

The Water of Leith passes through Dean Village in a deep cleft. Water extraction by industry has reduced its flow to a great extent. It was once sufficient to power 11 water mills producing meal for the town and surrounding villages, and giving rise to this settlement in the 12thC, known originally as the Village of the Water of Leith.

A satisfying counterbalance to the Georgian formality of the New Town, its intimacy and apparently random layout, enriched by trees and running water, reward those who leave the main road at Dean Bridge and explore. Many of the original buildings have been restored and converted into flats.

Dean Bridge   A3
An elegant series of spans by Thomas Telford, 1829–31. Look for the stone incorporated into Kirkbrae House at the north east corner, dated 1619 and bearing the inscription, taken from Genesis *In the sweat of thy face shalt thou eat bread*, and decorated with wheatsheaves, shovels and the sun. The 17thC house was once an inn, the Baxter's (Baker's) House of Call. The riverside walk to Leith starts below the bridge.

Baxter's Tolbooth   A3
At the foot of Bell Brae. Now restored, this was once the headquarters of the Incorporation of Bakers, and also their granary. An inscription reads *God Bless the Baxters of Edinburgh who built this hous (sic) 1675*. Look out for other inscribed stones nearby.

West Mill   A3
Standing by the 18thC stone bridge, this massive mill building, now converted into flats, is the only one which remains. The stone on its facade dated 1805 refers

to its rebuilding – it is known there was a mill on this site by 1573. When working, it was powered by two huge breast-wheels, 3.65m wide with a diameter of 5.48m.

Well Court   A3

Built 1883–6 for John Ritchie Findlay of *The Scotsman* newspaper at a cost of £14,000, and given to the village to compensate for loss of trade to other, larger mills. This is a thoroughly enjoyable collection of stair-turrets, corbelled windows and gables around a square, with a separate clock tower at one corner, once a community centre but now used, appropriately, as an architect's office. This picturesque development was conceived by Sydney Mitchell. A lane to the west leads to an ancient ford, with an iron footbridge alongside, and a riverside walk to Belford Bridge.

Dean Cemetery

Laid out by David Cousin on the site of Dean House in 1845, the home of the Nisbets of Dean from 1614 to 1827, there are many fine monuments to be seen here, notably those of Playfair, Lord Cockburn, Lord Rutherford, Lord Jeffrey et al. That to John Leishman is particularly striking. Belgrave Mews, at the entrance to the cemetery, stands on the site of the original Dean Village.

The Dean Village Community Association has produced an informative leaflet, available from Well Court (look on the notice board).

South
of the
Royal
Mile

George Heriot School

Old Edinburgh spilled southwards from the Royal Mile, its northerly expansion limited by the Nor' Loch, a source of drinking water and food (in the form of fish and eels), a place to dump rubbish, and ultimately a reservoir of disease until it was drained in the 1760s.

Much of the old spirit has left the medieval Grassmarket, but venture west along West Port and you may see some original tenement buildings before they are either demolished or refurbished. Walk south along the Vennel and you can see a part of the old City Wall, or climb up Candlemaker Row to explore the historic Greyfriars Kirk, surrounded by a most wonderful collection of tombs and stones. The statue of Greyfriars Bobby, that legendary loyal 'wee dug', stands just outside.

The Grassmarket   E5

The medieval Grassmarket, tucked in below the Castle and George Heriot's school, did not fare well from the improvements of 1840 and the mid 20thC. In fact it is hard to imagine how the more aggressive modern buildings of Heriot Watt University were allowed building permission. Granted its charter in 1477 by King James III a weekly market was held here until 1911 – a plaque at the west end commemorates the 500th anniversary of the charter. Main market day was Friday, when the place became so crowded it was impassable. Tanners and tobacconists, brewers and corn merchants, printers and makers of cat gut all plied their trade here, enlivened by visiting circuses and cock-fighting. The old water cistern still stands at the entrance to the West Bow, as does the White Hart Inn, a hostelry built at the end of the 18thC and frequented by the Highland cattle drovers and carriers, who came in cart or waggon at the rate of about 50 per week. Robert Burns stayed here for eight days in November 1791 on his last visit to Edinburgh, as did William Wordsworth, the poet.

The Grassmarket was also the scene of many public executions, one of the most notable involving Andrew Wilson, a smuggler, and Captain Porteous. Wilson, and his accomplice, Robertson, had both been condemned to death for robbing a customs house. While awaiting execution, it was usual for the prisoners to be taken to church on Sunday morning, under armed guard. In their case, Wilson and Robertson were taken to the Tolbooth Church. Seizing an opportunity, Robertson managed to escape cleanly into the crowd of church goers, and was last heard of in Holland. Wilson tried to follow, but was restrained, his struggles delaying the guard and thus helping his friend. Public sympathy was with the two condemned, and especially with Wilson, considered the worthier of the two characters. When the time of execution came, it was carried out by Captain Porteous, a man hated by the mob.

Following the hanging, the crowd grew restless, throwing stones and earth. Porteous, 'inflamed with wine' as Dr Alexander Carlyle, an eye witness, put it, ordered the Guard to fire on the crowd. Reluctantly they did so, but aimed high over their heads. People watching from windows were injured and one poor lad, Henry Black, was killed, along with seven or eight others.

Condemned to death himself, and then reprieved, Porteous was being held in the Tolbooth prison when the infuriated Edinburgh mob took him, dressed only in nightgown and slippers, in a torchlit procession back to the scene of Wilson's demise in the Grassmarket.

After obtaining rope, they tried to erect a gibbet, but to no avail. So they hung him from a dyester's pole and beat him with Lochaber axes and partisans (long handled spears), whilst the mob cheered. A St Andrew's Cross, in cobblestones within a small garden at the eastern end, marks the site of the gallows and an inscription reads, somewhat ironically, *For the Protestant faith on this spot many Martyrs and Covenanters died.* It was the Protestants who ordered the executions.

Other less formal, but equally gruesome happenings occurred in Tanners Close (off the Grassmarket, but now demolished). It was here that Messrs Burke and Hare enticed prostitutes and paupers to their rooms, strangled them, and sold the corpses to surgeons for medical research. It all eventually became too much for Hare, who confessed, and saved his life. Burke was hanged, in the Grassmarket, on 28 January 1829 before a crowd of 20,000. The judge who sentenced him said that his skeleton should be preserved 'in order that posterity may keep it in remembrance of your atrocious crimes'. His words were heeded, and his bones are kept at the Department of Anatomy, Edinburgh University.

It's more peaceful now, an area to browse among antiques and books, or relax in a pub or restaurant. Part of the old Flodden Wall, built around the city

after the disastrous defeat by the English at the Battle of Flodden Field in 1513, can be seen along the **Vennel**, a passage in the south west corner; if you walk along **West Port** there are still some unimproved (1987) tenement buildings, dated 1696, a grim reminder of what life was like for the poor of the city. Just up from the Grassmarket towards Greyfriars Church is **Candlemaker Row,** where the candlemakers were forced to settle in 1654. By the churchyard is Candlemakers Hall, a very handsome rubble-walled building by James Watson and dating from 1722. Note the moulded armorial panel above one of the doors. The craft of candlemaking, which had thrived in the city since 1488, met its demise with the introduction of gas lighting. The building was restored in 1929.

Greyfriars Kirk   F5

Built between 1602–20 in the garden of the old Greyfriars monastery, which was given to the town for use as a cemetery by Queen Mary in 1562. The original church was somewhat smaller than we see today, a plain nave with a tower at the west end.

Used as a barracks by Cromwell in 1650, all the original furnishings were destroyed. After being returned to ecclesiastical use in 1653, it suffered severe damage at a quarter to two in the morning of May 1718 when gunpowder stored in the tower by the city fathers exploded, once again leaving the congregation without a place of worship. Collections were taken in all the Edinburgh churches to pay for repairs, which were quickly executed by shortening the building, and constructing a new west wall and internal galleries to compensate for the lack of floor space. However, in November of the same year the Town Council decided to erect a new building adjoining the old one, creating a separate new church. This was completed in 1721 after demolishing the remains of the original tower. Fire seriously damaged old Greyfriars in 1845, and destroyed the furnishings of the new church. The new church was soon back in use, but restoration of the old church took longer.

In 1929 the two congregations united, with the dividing wall between the churches being demolished during the restoration of 1931–8. The result is the not very handsome building we see today. But if the church itself is of little interest, the events which took place here certainly are. For it was in the churchyard, on 28 February 1638 that the congregation, together with the merchants and nobles of Edinburgh, gathered to sign the Covenant and pledge themselves to oppose anyone trying to establish Roman Catholicism in Scotland. The Covenant also called for a free Scottish Parliament, supported Charles I but warned him against interference in the affairs of the church. Copies were signed, sometimes in blood, in churches throughout the country. When Charles II came to the throne, his attempt to put down Presbyterianism led to a revolt of the Covenanters. Edinburgh was torn by religious strife until the Covenanters were defeated at Bothwell Bridge in 1679. There followed 'The Killing Times' – persecution, torture and execution under the Duke of York. The exposed Covenanters Prison in the south west corner, which once had held 1200 for five winter months after the Battle of Bothwell Bridge, can still be seen in the churchyard, and the Martyrs Monument, backing onto Candlemaker Row, erected in 1706, should also be inspected. Part of the inscription reads:

Here lies interr'd the dust of those who stood
'Gainst perjury, resisting unto Blood,
Adhering to the Covenants and laws
Establishing the same: which was the cause
Their lives were sacrific'd unto the lust of
Prelatists abjur'd.

Ironically, the fine mausoleum of Sir George Mackenzie of Rosehaugh, 'Bluidy Mackenzie', is nearby. He was the Lord Advocate who ordered the torture and execution of many of the Covenanters buried in the churchyard, and was interred here in 1691. Indeed the whole churchyard, beautifully sited, is crammed full of magnificent monuments and ornamented tombstones, the finest 17thC collection in Scotland, and a haven of peace and quiet for those above the ground as well as those below. Edinburgh notables buried here include the architect William Adam; George Buchanan, Mary Queen of Scots' tutor; and architect of the New Town, James Craig. And of course, the grave of **Greyfriars Bobby** just inside the entrance, the famous 'wee dug' whose bronze model stands at the top of Candlemaker Row. The faithful friend of Border shepherd Jock Grey, he would not leave his master's grave in the churchyard. 'Arrested' for being unlicensed, he was reprieved when his street friends petitioned the Lord Provost. Given the Freedom of the City, and an engraved collar, Bobby lived happily until 1872. He now rests near his master, a gesture suggested by Queen Victoria herself, and one which the majority of visitors to Greyfriars still find more alluring then the bloody episode in Scotland's history which began, and ended, here.

George Heriot's School   E6

An imposing building of towers and turrets on a very prominent site south of the Castle. Built as the result of a bequest of £23,625 by George Heriot, royal goldsmith and banker, work began in 1628 and, after faltering when money failed to materialise, it was substantially finished

Royal Residences

Above right: **Edinburgh Castle**

Below: **Palace of Holyroodhouse**

The
Royal Mile

Far left: **View from the Castle of Esplanade and Tolbooth Church**

Below left: **Royal Arms of Scotland above Castle entrance**

Centre: **Ramsay Gardens**

Below right: **White Horse Close**

Viewpoints

Above left: **Festival cavalcade**

Below left: **Castle from the Grassmarket**

Centre: **Edinburgh skyline from Calton Hill**

Above right: **Glenlivet firework display over the Castle**

Below right: **Greyfriars Bobby**

New Town

Above left: **Sir Walter Scott's monument, Princes Street**

Centre: **Dean Village**

Below: **Charlotte Square**

Village Edinburgh

Above left: **Leith**
Centre: **Cramond Harbour**
Below: **Duddingston**

A Day Out of Town

Above right: **St Andrews Cathedral**

Centre: **Linlithgow Palace**

Below: **Forth Rail Bridge**

by 1648. Later work included the completion of the chapel in 1673, and the building of the octagonal dome and lantern in 1693.

This hospital, as it was first known, was in fact a charity school. The first beneficiaries, thirty boys, were finally accepted in 1659, the delay occasioned by Cromwell's occupation of the building, which was used as a hospital for the wounded after the Battle of Dunbar, 1650.

It was on 5 October 1785 at 14.45 from the grounds of the school that the great Vincenzo Lunardi made his flight in a hydrogen filled balloon. Dressed in a uniform of scarlet and blue, and idolised by the young ladies of Edinburgh (who he found much to his liking) he rose to a height of 335m and drifted slowly over the Forth to land at Ceres in Fife at 16.20. He was promptly made a freemason of the nearby burgh of St Andrews and a member of the Society for Gentlemen Golfers. The ladies of neighbouring Cupar mended his balloon and later, upon his return to Edinburgh, he was also made a Freeman of the City. The school looks its best when framed in the gateway to St Giles' churchyard.

Edinburgh University   F6
The university is the largest private owner of buildings in Scotland, and many are to be found to the south of the Old Town, in the area around George Square. This predominantly white middle class seat of learning, with over 11,000 students, has achieved an enviable reputation in the fields of science and medicine, and many highly advanced and technological research projects (viz. School of Artificial Intelligence) are undertaken within its walls.

Founded under the royal charter of James VI in 1583, some of the spirit of the strict Calvinistic principles imposed then still survive today. The original university building was built on the corner of Chamber's Street and South Bridge, where its replacement building, still confusingly referred to as the Old College, now stands. Enclosing a quad, the exterior is by Robert Adam 1789, the interior by William H. Playfair 1819–27. There has never been one complex of colleges but rather a disparate assortment of buildings each with its own discipline. The original faculties were General Arts and Divinity, with Medicine and Law being added in 1705 and 1722, and others following.

Notable among chancellors here have been John Buchan, James Barrie and HRH the Duke of Edinburgh; elected representatives, or rectors, have included Prime Ministers William Ewart Gladstone, Lord Rosebery, David Lloyd George, Stanley Baldwin and Winston Churchill (who was not chosen during his first election of 1905). Famous among the students have been Lord Palmerston, Charles Darwin, and writers James Boswell, Thomas Carlyle, Sir Arthur Conan Doyle, Sir Walter Scott and Robert Louis Stevenson.

The McEwan Hall, Teviot Place. One of Edinburgh University's most remarkable buildings. Built to a 'D' plan, it stands like a glorious and elaborately iced cake topped by a gentle dome and lantern. It was built in 1897 by Sir R. Rowand Anderson who used the traditional form of ancient Greek theatre as his model. A lengthy echo tends to restrict its use as a concert hall.

Surgeons Hall, Nicolson St. One of William H. Playfair's Greek temples, built 1829–32 and restored circa 1960.

Heriot-Watt University
Obtained university status in 1966. It was founded in 1821 as an evening class school in basic science. It is now largely situated at Riccarton on the outskirts of the city.

Parks, Gardens and Viewpoints

Ross Fountain, Princes Street Gardens

It is often said that Edinburgh is a city built upon seven hills, like Rome. But in truth Edinburgh has given its summits to the builders of castles and monuments, leaving them for the most part green and, in some cases, surprisingly wild, as Dorothy Wordsworth discovered when she climbed Arthur's Seat on 6 September 1803:

'We set out upon our walk, and went through many streets to Holyroodhouse, and thence to the hill called Arthur's Seat, a high hill, very rocky at the top, and below covered with smooth turf, on which sheep were feeding. We climbed up till we came to St Anthony's Well and Chapel, a small ruin, which from its situation is extremely interesting, though in itself not remarkable. We sat down on a stone not far from the chapel, overlooking a pastoral hollow as wild and solitary as any in the heart of the Highland mountains: there, instead of the roaring of torrents, we listened to the noises of the city, which were blended in one loud indistinct buzz – a regular sound in the air, which in certain moods of feeling, and at certain times, might have a more tranquillizing effect upon the mind than those which we are accustomed to hear in such places. Though the rain was very heavy we remained upon the hill for some time.'

It is surprising how little has changed.

Scottish Zoological Park

Corstorphine Rd. 031–334 9171. Founded in the grounds of Corstorphine Hill House in 1913 by Thomas Gillespie and planned by Sir Patrick Geddes, the zoo has always pioneered the principle of keeping animals in surroundings that are as natural as possible. The success of this is seen by the number of species, and particularly endangered species, which are breeding here. Indeed it is pleasing to note that the Scottish Zoological Society is decreasing the number of animals kept purely for display, and is concentrating on those which can be sustained as breeding groups. Education and research go hand in hand with the obvious pleasure that seeing animals can bring. The modest entrance gives little clue to the superb 80 acre sloping site upon which the zoo is built.

There are over 2000 animals to see, and each species is identified by a board giving its name (common and Latin), description, distribution, habitat, diet and behaviour. Keep an eye out for the

rare pygmy hippopotomus; Maxwell's duiker, a shy forest living antelope from West Africa; the guanaco a wild ancestor of the llama and a pair of snow leopards, which are a seriously endangered species from the foothills of the Himalayas. There is a newly designed chimpanzee house with a termite mound. Wild chimps fashion sticks into tools for poking into termite nests. The termites crawl up the sticks and the chimps lick them off. The artificial mound contains not termites but honey which the chimps may dip for. The African plains exhibit is an important feature of Edinburgh Zoo. It is a large undulating area with trees practically on the summit of Zoo Hill, an ideal mixed herd species exhibit. The view of the animals is unimpeded due to a hidden ha-ha ditch and one can watch the interaction amongst groups of zebra, oryx and lechwe antelope. A whole day is barely time enough to see everything, but things to particularly look out for, apart from your favourite animals, are:
Penguin parade – *Apr–Sep* 14.30
Feeding the sea lions – *Apr–Sep* 15.00
Animal handling sessions – when visi-

tors can touch snake eggs, snakes, geckos, toads, frogs and so on – Easter and summer school holidays, 13.00 and 13.30. Book at the bookshop, small extra charge.

If you get tired of peering at animals, there is an adventure playground for the children, brass rubbing at the Children's Farm, mask making, or you could just climb up to the highest point and enjoy the view of the city. The car park is behind the Trust House Forte Post House Hotel next to the zoo. Hot meals and snacks are available in the Penguin's Pantry, which is licensed. In the summer the Den is also open, selling cold drinks. Picnics can be enjoyed on the many grassy areas around the zoo or in the picnic area adjoining the Steading. A limited number of wheelchairs are available at the main gate (folding pushchairs only will go through the turn stiles). An excellent natural history bookshop adjoins the education unit and stocks books, posters and cards. The zoo gift shop is opposite and sells souvenirs. Enter by main gate only. No dogs. *Open 09.00–18.00 Mon–Sat; 09.30–18.00 Sun. Closes at 17.00 or dusk in winter. Admission charge.*

Blackford Hill

(164m). A pleasant climb through parkland will reward you with one of the finest panoramas of the city, seen over the leafy southern suburbs with the Forth and the distant shores of Fife beyond. To the east Salisbury Crags and Arthur's Seat command the skyline. Turn through 180° and there is unspoilt countryside on the slopes of the Pentland Hills. The Royal Observatory building dates from 1892 (see Museums, page 136). Three years later the Astronomer Royal moved here to escape the smoke which obscured the view from Calton Hill, recalling Edinburgh's nick-name of 'Auld Reekie' (old smoky). Between the

domed telescope towers are panels decorated with the signs of the Zodiac.

Calton Hill   H2

(100m). An intimate view of the city skyline, crowned by the Castle. To the north is the Forth and the Kingdom of Fife, best seen from the top of the Nelson monument. All the monuments are described on page 57.

Castle Hill   D4

(133m). Bird's-eye view over Princes Street, through the Scott monument and Calton Hill to the Royal Mile.

Corstorphine Hill

(162m). Rising above the zoo, it is a fine walk along the crest of the hill, with the city laid out below. The Hill Tower was built in 1871 by William Macfie of Dreghorn, and commemorates the centenary of the birth of Sir Walter Scott.

Holyrood Park

Rising to a height of 251m at **Arthur's Seat,** the igneous core of an extinct volcano, Holyrood Park remains surprisingly wild in spite of the city that has spread around it. There were four prehistoric hill forts here, and evidence of cultivation terraces, dating from the Dark Ages, have been found on the eastern slopes of Arthur's Seat. There are two lochs, Dunsapie and St Margaret's: it is by the latter that the remains of St Anthony's Chapel can be seen. Of late medieval date, its origins are not known. **Salisbury Crags** provide a magnificently precipitous backdrop for the Palace of Holyroodhouse: below them were the Wells o'Wearie, where the hapless trudged for water when the city's supply failed.

The walk to Arthur's Seat is not difficult, with a well defined path up from Dunsapie Loch. If you are there at dawn on the first of May, you can witness a religious service, a tradition revived after the Second World War by the Rev Selby-Wright of Canongate.

The Meadows   F7

A pleasant area to the south of the university and hospital buildings, where, in 1886, the International Exhibition of Industry, Science and Art was held. This great extravaganza took place in a massive building of brick and steel covering seven acres. Intended as a permanent structure it had to be dismantled when an Act of Parliament forbidding building on the Meadows was discovered. It was intended to rival the Great Exhibition held at Crystal Palace, London, some five years earlier, and it did not fall far short. It was visited by Queen Victoria on 18 August, and closed on 30 October with a magnificent firework display. It had cost £40,000, had been seen by two and a half million visitors, and made a profit of £20,000.

There are reminders of this great show still to be seen: two stone pillars, 8m tall, either side of Melville Drive at the Tollcross end, were the main entrance, their 18 courses of stone each coming from a different quarry; the whalebone arch at the entrance of Jawbone walk, presented by the Shetland Fair Isle Knitting Stand; and a lonely sundial at the west end, to commemorate the opening on 5 May by Queen Victoria's grandson, Prince Albert Victor.

Princes Street Gardens   D4

These gardens, on the site of the drained Nor' Loch, which was infilled with excavations from the building of the New Town, are now a favourite lunchtime venue for the city's workers, strolling tourists and sunbathers on fine summer days. Bounded by Princes Street to the north, and the Castle and the Old Town to the south, its situation is superb.

Although one can understand the disquiet caused when the railway was built, it now seems to intrude much less than would seem possible.

The gardens, noted for their floral clock display, are firmly divided into two parts by The Mound (see page 54). The Scott Monument (described in detail on page 54) dominates East Princes Street Gardens, but also have a look at the bronze statue of David Livingstone (1813–1873) close by. He was a Scottish explorer who discovered the course of the Zambesi River, Victoria Falls and Lake Nyasa (now Lake Malawi) and was a vociferous opponent of slavery. Believed lost, he was found by explorer Sir Henry Morton Stanley on 10 November 1871.

Once there were proposals to build Waverley Station under a grassed roof, thus re-instating the area of park it occupied, but these came to no avail.

West Princes Street Gardens sit directly beneath the Castle – indeed at one time they extended around its base as far as the Grassmarket. Naturally, the gardens are well endowed with statues and monuments.

Allan Ramsay (1686–1758), the Edinburgh poet, stands carved in Carrara marble in the north east corner above the renowned floral clock. Opposite Frederick Street, on a rocky pedestal, stands the superb and realistic figure of a Royal Scots Greys Trooper, cast in bronze by Birnie Rhind in 1906. His subject was Sergeant-Major Anthony James Hinnigan (1866–1931) of Jedburgh, who served for 29 years, and was injured during the Boer War. Following his discharge he ran the Railway Inn in Irvine. The name of his horse was 'Polly'.

Dr Thomas Guthrie, founder of the Ragged Schools, stands bible in hand opposite Castle Street. Other works are Sir James Simpson; the Scottish American War Memorial, the more modern

Royal Botanic Gardens

Arboretum Road and Inverleith Row.
031–552 7171. Occupies an area of 70
acres less than a mile north of Princes
Street. These gardens are the
culmination of work begun by Dr Robert
Sibbald, the first Professor of Medicine
at Edinburgh University, and Dr Robert
Balfour, who established a physic
garden, just 12m square, on a site near
Holyrood in 1670. There they grew
medicinal plants and herbs. However,
they soon needed more space, and six
years later took over the Trinity Hospital
garden, on a site now occupied by
Waverley Station. James Sutherland was
appointed to care for both gardens; he
rapidly became Edinburgh's leading
botanist, being made Professor of
Botany at the University in 1695, and
ultimately Regius Professor of Botany in
1710.

His successor, John Hope, who had
studied at the Royal Garden in Paris,
continued the development, moving to a
larger five acre site where Haddington
Place (Leith Walk) now stands.
Furthermore he secured a permanent
income from the Crown for the gardens.
Also made Regius Professor, he
encouraged his students to research and
investigate Scottish plant life, arranging
plant collecting not only on the mainland
but on Orkney, Shetland and the
Western Isles as well.

Daniel Rutherford followed in 1786,
a man more interested in plants as a
means to his chemical experiments, but
who was fortunate in having some
exceptional head gardeners, including
John Tweedie, who introduced some
exotic plants – verbena and Chilean
jasmine; John McKay, who exchanged
plants with the botanic gardens at Kew;
and William McNab, who came from
Kew and introduced many rare plants
and specialised in aquatics, introducing

species from all around the world. But
perhaps his greatest success was in
organising the move to the present site
at Inverleith, a complex and difficult task
spread over two years, during which
time he lost hardly a single plant or tree.

In 1864 the Experimental Garden of
the Royal Caledonian Horticultural
Society was transferred here, and 12
years later the grounds surrounding
Inverleith House were added. During the
latter part of the 19thC under Isaac
Bayley Balfour the Edinburgh Botanic
Gardens became an important centre for
taxology (classification of living things),
especially with regard to the plants of
China and the Himalayas. George Forrest
made seven trips to western China and
brought back thousands of specimens
which contributed to this work.

At the end of the 19thC the gardens
were transferred to the Treasury to the
First Commissioner of Works and were,
for the first time, opened to the public on
Sundays. As you would expect, the Free
Presbyterian Church declared it 'a
wanton desecration'. None of that
'closer to God in a garden' nonsense for
them. Now it is open every day, for
everyone to enjoy.

The Rhododendron Walk

The largest collection of rhododendrons
in Britain begins near the West Gate, a
mass of colour in the spring and early
summer. Magnolias blossom on the east
side of Inverleith House, with other
plants, hellibores and mahonias
providing colour into the winter.

The Copse

An informal woodland garden, where
native trees and hedges provide shelter
for less hardy foreign species, magnolias
and lilies. A superb herbaceous border
provides vibrant colour and perfume.

Parks, Gardens and Viewpoints

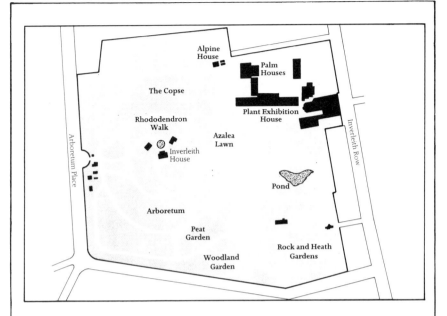

Look out for the magnificent Monterey cypress. To the north is the demonstration garden, a fount of ideas for the amateur gardener.

Plant Exhibition Houses
Superb all the year round but especially pleasant in winter, when the warm, balmy, scented atmosphere provides a welcome retreat from the penetrating east wind. Cacti and succulents, tropical waterlilies, Amazonion lilies, tree ferns, orchids and cycads, tropical peat and rock plants are all found here.

The Palm Houses
The Tropical Palm House was opened in 1834 and contains, amidst a wealth of specimens, a West Indian thatch palm over 170 years old, successfully transplanted from Haddington Place by William McNab, using his special tree moving machine. It fruits in May. The Temperate Palm House was built in 1858, and is also full to the roof with an outstanding variety of plants and trees.

Alpine House
In here will be found the more tender alpines, primulas, saxifrages and the like, with one or more in flower.

Azalea Lawn
A blaze of colour and richly perfumed, azaleas come into flower during May. Beech and birch trees provide a back drop.

The Pond
A habitat for aquatic and moisture loving plants. Outstanding is the Gunnera manicata, the largest leaved hardy plant grown in Britain – in a favourable year the leaves of this rhubarb-like plant measure 1.5m across. The water also attracts bird and animal life.

Rock and Heath Gardens
James McNab, a leading horticulturist from Kew Gardens, constructed the Rock Garden in 1871, using plants from Europe, China, Japan, India, Australia and North and South America. Some of

71

the basaltic stone was brought from the island of Staffa, to the west of Mull. Conifers and junipers are also incorporated. The Heath Garden was created in 1935, and you will always find heathers in bloom here, whatever the time of year.

Woodland Garden

The wildest part of the Botanic Gardens, much loved by children.

The Peat Garden

The first of its kind in Britain, created in 1939 by William Wright Smith, it not unnaturally provides unique conditions for peat-loving plants such as primulas, gentians and dwarf rhododendrons.

Shrubs provide frost protection for lilies and orchids.

The Arboretum

A rich collection of trees, where native species have been skilfully planted to provide shelter for less hardy imports.

Gardens open 09.00–sunset Mon–Sat; 11.00–sunset Sun. (NB gardens close 1 hour before sunset during British summer time). Plant Houses and Exhibition Hall: open 10.00–17.00 Mon–Sat; 11.00–17.00 Sun. Inverleith House, Gallery and Visitor Centre: open Apr–Sep, times as for Plant Houses. Admission free.

Royal Scots Memorial and the Statuary Group. Also look out for the Ross Fountain, cast in Paris for the International Exhibition of 1862, and described as 'grossly indecent and disgusting' by Dean Ramsay when erected here. There is also a rune stone of circa 1200 by the walk beneath the Castle Esplanade. It originated from Sweden. In 1987 it was decided to erect a memorial to Robert Louis Stevenson, on the centenary of his death. The design, by Ian Hamilton Finlay, takes the form of a sacred grove, with five birch trees, but at the time of writing, the site within the gardens is uncertain.

Village Edinburgh

Leith

One of the great advantages of Edinburgh is its compactness and accessibility, with all the major sights, plus a wealth of shops, restaurants and pubs crammed into little more than a square mile at the centre. But outside this area are a series of villages which have retained their unique identities in spite of the inevitable urban sprawl. Dean Village and Stockbridge are two such places, indeed they are especially remarkable for being so close to the centre, and have for this reason been described along with the New Town. Venture a little further afield and you will add a surprising dimension to your view of the capital city.

Colinton
Buses: 5/51, 9, 10, 32/52, 71. Train: to Slateford.

The Water of Leith Walkway passes the beautiful wooded glades of Colinton and Craiglockhart Dell, separated from the foothills of the Pentlands by the new by-pass. The old village of Colinton sits tucked into the valley on the south western outskirts of the city, but the industries that were once its life-blood, farming, papermaking and grain milling, disappeared during the late 19thC industrial decline. To take its place came Victorian and Edwardian commuters, who followed the building of the railway in 1875 and built their fine villas on the higher ground. The parish church of **St Cuthbert's**, which underwent some alterations in 1907–8, dates from 1771, replacing an earlier building of 1650. To the left of the entrance gates is an old mort safe, a device once used to prevent bodies being dug up for medical research. Buried in the churchyard are Rev Dr Lewis Balfour, once minister here and grandfather to Robert Louis Stevenson, and James Gillespie, mill owner and benefactor to the famous school. Indeed, Stevenson spent much time at his grandfather's manse, mentioning it, and the old yew tree, in *Kidnapped*. The ivy covered ruin of the 16thC **Colinton Castle** stands now in the grounds of Merchiston Castle School. The castle was vandalised by Cromwell's men in 1650, repaired, then rendered a romantic ruin on the instructions of artist Alexander Nasmyth in 1804. **Colinton House**, built 1801–6, is now the science block of the school. The 15thC **Merchiston Tower,** birthplace of the distinguished mathematician John Napier, has been incorporated into the new buildings of Napier College. Fine mansions, humble cottages, old mills, a handsome church and tumbling water in the Dell make this ideal for an afternoon stroll.

Corstorphine
Buses: 2/12, 16, 26

The centrepiece of this village is the 15thC old **Parish Church** standing amidst a fine array of gravestones. In the south chapel is the monument to Sir Adam Forrester who died in 1405. Lord Provost of Edinburgh, he bought the estate in 1376 and built a chapel here. Nothing remains of his castle building but the dovecot, which housed 1060 nests.

Farming, and later market gardening, supported the village for

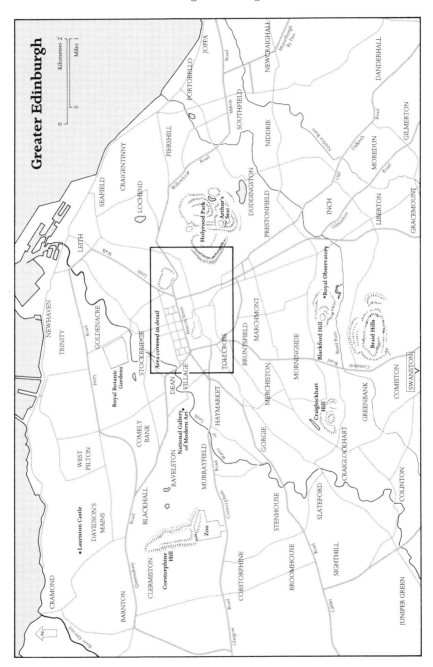

Greater Edinburgh

many years, with a short period as a spa town until the sulphurous spring became polluted. If you are travelling on the Glasgow Road to the west of the city, a short stop here by the church in Kirk Loan is worthwhile. Under the slopes of Corstorphine Hill lies the Scottish Zoological Park.

Cramond
Buses: 18, 41.

Cramond **Parish Church** was built in 1656 to replace an earlier medieval building, itself built on the site of a **Roman fort** established here in 142 AD by Antonius Pius, and used as a base when building the Antonine Wall. Excavations in the mid 1950s revealed the outline of the Roman buildings, which can be seen around the church today. But the real reason for venturing this far to the north west of the city centre is Cramond's superb situation where the River Almond enters the Forth. It is postcard pretty. Eighteenth-century workers' houses have been tastefully restored, and in the summer yachts bob gently at their moorings by the quay. There are excellent walks along the foreshore to the Forth Bridge (4½ miles) with a breezy views of the estuary and **Cramond Island**. You can walk upstream beside the River Almond, past the remains of water-driven mills which once ground meal and later became the forge for an ironworks, to finish at the old **Cramond Bridge**. It was here that James I, on his way to Perth in 1436, was warned to go no further by a soothsayer. He ignored the warning, and was murdered. James V was attacked on the bridge, being saved by Jock Howison, a miller. In gratitude the King gave Howison the land around Braehead, on condition there should always be an ewer of water and a basin ready for the reigning monarch. One of Howison's descendants upheld this tradition when he presented Elizabeth II with a silver ewer and a bowl of rose water. The Cramond Inn is a picturesque pub and restaurant. The Cramond Heritage Trust has opened an interpretive centre in the Old Maltings, by the quay.

Duddingston
Buses: 4, 42/46.

Nestling in the shadow of Arthur's Seat, the enclosed, almost feudal, village of Duddingston occupies the higher ground to the north of

Duddingston Loch (nature reserve and bird sanctuary). A cottage industry, the weaving of flaxen cloth known as 'hardings', flourished here in the early 18thC, then gradually gave way to milling, brewing and work in the pits.

Much of the **church** dates from the 12thC, and contains some fine original Norman work. The tower is a later 17thC addition. High rubble walls seem to predominate; these defined the boundaries of the grounds of **Duddingston House**, a superb 18thC villa built by William Chambers for the eighth Earl of Abercorn and now used as a hotel, with much of the park given over to golf.

The **Sheep Heid Inn** on the Causeway stands on the site of an earlier building visited by James VI, who presented the landlord with a decorated ram's head in 1580. **Number 8, the Causeway** is said to be the house where Bonnie Prince Charlie stayed before his victory over the Royalists at the Battle of Prestonpans in 1745.

Less than two miles from Holyrood, and separated only by parkland, Duddingston village is the ideal destination for a walk from the city centre.

Leith

Buses: 2/12, 7, 10, 16, 25.

The natural harbour formed where the Water of Leith enters the Forth gave rise to the settlement here, which became Edinburgh's port in 1329. Indeed so successful did Leith become as a trading centre, that in 1413 Edinburgh secured a charter from Sir Robert Logan of Restalrig, owner of the lands on the east side of the river, restricting the port's ability to trade separately from the city. Development on the west bank began in 1493 with the building of a bridge, and the founding of St Ninian's Chapel, the site of which is now occupied by granary buildings incorporating a later belfry. In 1548 Mary of Guise established the seat of Government here, and built fortifications, but the Protestant siege of 1560 destroyed the walls and re-asserted the superiority of Edinburgh. Leith's independent trade guilds continued to flourish however, and rivalry between the city and its upstart port continued until Leith gained burgh status in 1833, finally losing it once and for all in 1920. A brass plaque halfway along Leith Walk marks the old boundary.

During the 18thC Leith became a fashionable resort, with a golf course and bathing machines. Regular streets lined with elegant villas began to intrude upon and enclose the old pell mell development.

Most of old Leith was pulled down following the introduction of the Leith Improvement Act of 1880, and this ethos continued well into the 20thC. What has replaced the old is of little merit. Expansion of the harbour facilities was given an impetus by the Earl of Hertford, who built a wooden pier in 1544 during his invasion. During the 17th and 18thC wharves and dry docks were built and then extended. The first deep water dock was built in 1806, with further docks and piers following to the extent that they bankrupted the City of Edinburgh in 1833 (which presumably caused the granting of separate burgh status to Leith). Building continued into the first half of this century, with the deep water harbour at Newhaven (see below) being incorporated in 1936–43. It is also worth noting that ship building was once an important industry – *Sirius*, the first British steam ship to cross the Atlantic, was built here in 1837. Today Leith is an intriguing mixture of old and new, streets lined with tall warehouses, the salty tang of a harbour and a flush of new restaurants and wine bars. The **Customs House**, built 1810–12, still stands massively in Commercial Street, and there is a Maritime Museum in **Trinity House**, in Kirkgate.

Leith confirms Edinburgh's status as a port – a city by the sea – and none the worse for that.

Morningside

Buses: 11, 15, 16, 41.

Morningside has been a well-to-do and growing suburb since the advent of the railways in the mid 19thC. It is a salubrious area and leads up to the slopes of the Braid Hills.

Initially the hub of the village was around the area now occupied by the Public Library and the Merlin pub. The influx of the wealthy expanded the village far beyond the original centre, with their elegant villas. Only a few of these buildings remain including the home of the Misses Balfour, aunts of Robert Louis Stevenson. However, some of the old stone cottages still stand in **Springvalley Terrace**. Look out for **Braid Road**, the scene of public executions marked by two large square stones with holes to support the gibbets. Go into the Volunteer's Arms, on the corner of Canaan and Morningside Lanes, and you will find a complete range of copper whisky blending jugs and measures as well as an old account book. As for the accent, that is said to have derived from the Irish elecutionist, Thomas Sheridan, father of the famous playwright.

Today Morningside is a spacious suburb, which retains some of the well-to-do air of the turn of the century.

Newhaven

Buses: 7, 10, 11, 16.

Now the westerly continuation of Leith, but once, during the reign of James IV, it was an important ship-building village, where the flagship of the Scottish navy, the *Great Michael*, was built by Flemish, Dutch and French workers in 1511. During the 17th–19thC, when its importance waned in the shadow of its more powerful neighbours, it became a fishing village, famous for its colourful fish-wives whose cries rang through the narrow lanes.

'Wha'll buy my caller herrin'?
They're bonnie fish an' halesome farin',
Wha'll buy my caller herrin'
New drawn frae the Forth?'

Newhaven's reputation for seafood was such that a market was established here in 1896, when a bowl of oysters could be had for 2½p. Today the attractive harbour is a safe haven for pleasure craft.

The old Newhaven that still survives, on the Main Street, and in Lamb's Court, Fishmarket Square and Peacock Court has been carefully restored, and one or two fine old inns invite a visit. There is a good local museum in Victoria School, in the Main Street.

Portobello

Buses: 2/12, 15, 26, 42/46.

Like a faded and forgotten star of the music hall, Portobello lies to the east of the city yearning for the return of the good old days. But public tastes are fickle, and regrettably what amused the Victorians and Edwardians no longer appeals to us.

After Admiral Vernon had defeated the Spanish at the Battle of Puerto Bello in Panama in 1739, one of his sailors returned home and built a small thatched cottage which he named Porto Bello, where the Baptist Church now stands in the High Street. Some 20 years later an Edinburgh builder bought a further 40 acres of the Brunstane Estate, built seven large villas and a brickworks. His name was William Jamieson, and he was known as the 'Father of Portobello'. Another entrepreneur, John Cairns, advertised bathing machines on the sands in the late 18thC, when bracing salt winds and sea bathing were fashionable for their therapeutic effects. Modest Georgian villas were followed by more elaborate Victorian houses. A pier fully 381m long with a concert hall and restaurant at the end was built. Steamers called for trips to Fife. The Portobello Marine Gardens opened in 1910, followed by the Empress Ballroom, concert hall, cinema and a massive funfair. Dare devils dived 20m into small pools, balloon ascents were made and in 1912 W.R. Ewan landed his flying machine on the beach. Trippers came in their thousands to visit the 'Queen of the Forth'.

Then it all went wrong. By 1950 the golden sands were gone, replaced by filth. The massive outdoor swimming pool, opened in 1936 and supposedly warmed by spare heat from the power station next door, and which had once seen 18,000 bathers in one day, attracted barely more than that in a whole year. It is now closed. Portobello will never regain its past glory, but the re-sanding of the beach carried out in the 1970s has been successful, and the air is as bracing as ever it was. Some of the elegant villas are still to be seen around Bath Street. It's worth a visit. And music hall stars? Harry Lauder was born in a cottage in Portobello in 1870. It's number **3 Bridge Street**. There are fine, breezy walks along the foreshore.

Swanston
Bus 4 to Oxgang Rd, then walk.

At the end of Swanston Road, a half a mile outside the new southern by-pass and surrounded by open fields and golf courses, the group of thatched 17thC cottages, the farmhouse and the school which comprise Swanston seem remarkably rural. Separated from this group, beyond some 19thC farmworkers' houses, is Swanston Cottage, built in 1761 and used by Robert Louis Stevenson's family as a holiday home between 1867 and 1880. His beloved nanny, Alison Cunningham, owned one of the houses nearby. The Pentland Hills rise gently to the south.

A Day in Town

Sir Walter Scott's Monument

81

Only in Edinburgh for a day or two? Don't worry. Promise yourself that you will stay for longer next time, then use the following itineraries to get the most from your short stay. You will not, of course, see everything, but the fact that Edinburgh is so compact means you can get the flavour of Scotland's capital, without spending too much time travelling.

For simplicity each walking tour starts at Waverley Station, bang in the middle, and definitely the best way to arrive in the city, with no parking problems. The schedules allow for brief visits to the places mentioned – clearly if you linger at one place, another visit will have to be shortened, or missed altogether. And remember that most historic buildings and museums close around 17.00.

The National Trust for Scotland owns over a 100 properties in Edinburgh and the rest of Scotland. If you are planning to visit more than three or four of these during the course of a year, especially if you are a family group, you can save money by becoming a member and enjoying the benefit of unlimited free admission. You will also be admitted free to a further three hundred properties in the rest of the British Isles. You can usually join at a NTS property or you can write for a leaflet to: National Trust for Scotland, 5 Charlotte Square, Edinburgh EH2 4DU.

Details of your route and sights to see are given here (complete descriptions can be found elsewhere in the book). A street plan will be found on pages 156–157. If you are in Edinburgh for one day only, choose which itinerary appeals most, for two days, tackle both!

Finally, for those who do not wish to walk far, there are some suggestions for seeing the sights in a more leisurely fashion.

Walk 1

Combines a visit to the Castle with a taste of both the Old and New Towns

09.30
Scott Monument – climb to the top for a great view of the city. Completed in 1846, one of Scotland's best loved writers sits carved in marble with his dog Maida at his side beneath this elaborate memorial.

10.00
Cross Princes Street to admire Jenners department store, a beautiful Renaissance building completed in 1895. Visit

the food hall for a packet of shortbread to sustain you throughout the morning.

10.30
Walk up St David Street to Thistle Street on your left. Just around the corner you will see the first two houses to be built in the New Town, dating from 1768.

10.45
Carry on along St David Street, turn right into Queen Street to visit the National

Museum of Antiquities, where there is an intriguing array of archaeological exhibits. After admiring the Gothic entrance hall, look out for the Lewis chessmen, the Traprain silver and the Monymusk Reliquary.

11.45
Retrace your steps past St Andrew Square, Scotland's financial heart, turn right along Princes Street then left up The Mound, passing the classical Greek temples which house the Royal Scottish Academy and National Gallery. There is usually a lone piper on the corner here – the Rev Alan Cameron, piper and preacher. Turn right into Mound Place and climb Ramsay Lane to the Castle.

12.00
There has been a fortification here since the 6thC AD, with the oldest building, St Margaret's Chapel, dating from the 12thC. Enjoy the superb views.

13.00
Return to the Mills Mount Battery overlooking Princes Street to see (and hear) the firing of the one o'clock gun (weekdays only).

13.15
Try the Castle Tea Room, or the Ensign Ewart or Jolly Judge pubs (down Castlehill in the Lawnmarket) for lunch. Victoria Street and the Grassmarket are also good places to find refreshment.

14.15
Walk down the Royal Mile to the Palace of Holyroodhouse. On the way look out for: Gladstone's Land, an old merchant's house in the Lawnmarket, and definitely worth a look if you have the time; Lady Stair's House opposite; St Giles' Cathedral; Parliament Square and John Knox House Museum.

15.15
The present Palace of Holyroodhouse is little altered since it was rebuilt by Charles II in 1671. Amongst the rooms open to the general public are the picture gallery and the former apartments of Lord Darnley and Mary Queen of Scots.

16.15
Beyond the Palace is Holyrood Abbey of which the walls of the Chapel Royal are all that remain standing. The gardens and park are also worth exploring.

17.00
Walk up White Horse Close, the Royal Mews in the 16thC. Jacobite officers used the inn as headquarters in the 1745 rebellion. Walk on into Calton Road, which takes you back to the east end of Princes Street and Waverley Market.

Walk 2

Contrasts the Georgian elegance of the New Town with the ancient charm of Greyfriars churchyard and includes a walk through Princes Street Gardens and a visit to the Dean Village.

09.30
Walk through East Princes Street Gardens stopping to see the statue of David Livingstone (1813–1873), Scotland's most famous explorer and a vociferous opponent of slavery. Continue past the National Gallery of Scotland and cross the Mound into West Princes Street Gardens. The statue of Alan Ramsay (1686–1758), the Edinburgh poet, stands on the corner of Princes Street. In summer the gardens are alive with flowers, with the star attraction being the floral clock.

Continue walking through the gardens, but stop to admire the superb figure of a Royal Scots Greys Trooper, which was cast in 1906. The trooper was modelled on Sergeant Major Anthony

James Hinnigan and his horse Polly.

Further on is the Ross Fountain, which was cast in Paris. The voluptuous semi-naked figures were described as 'grossly indecent and digusting' when it was first erected here in 1864.

The gardens are dominated by the Castle, perched high above on the Castle Crag. The tall pink and cream turreted building at the foot of the Castle Esplanade is Ramsay Gardens, built as a hall of residence and flats 1892–4.

10.30

Two fine churches mark the west end of the gardens, St John's, a handsome building dating from 1818, and the remarkably picturesque St Cuthbert's, built in 1895 on the site of an earlier medieval building. Now cross Princes Street, walk up South Charlotte Square and then left into Charlotte Square itself. Look across to admire the frontage of one of Robert Adam's masterpieces. On the west side of the square, in the converted St George's Church, is the small permanent museum of the Scottish Record Office. Call in to see documents relating to The Declaration of Arbroath (which dates from 1320 and expresses Scottish devotion to Robert Bruce), The 'Auld Enemy' (England), The National Covenant and The Treaty of Union.

11.15

Now walk to the north side to visit number 7, the superb Georgian House. Designed by Robert Adam in 1791 and completed following his death in 1792 by Robert Reid. Inside you will find it furnished in the style of a wealthy family living during the reign of George III. It is one of Edinburgh's major attractions, and deservedly so.

12.45

Lunch. One of Edinburgh's most civilised retreats is Kay's Bar, in Jamaica Street, which you will find by walking north to Queen Street, turn left into Wemyss Place, right into Heriot Row, left into India Street and right into Jamaica Street. Otherwise there are several eating places around Edinburgh's West End.

13.45

Return to India Street, walk north to North West Circus Place and on to the Water of Leith. Do not cross the river but follow the waterside walkway eastwards to Dean Village.

14.15

Explore Dean Village, a very pretty cluster of buildings in a deep cleft. There were once 11 watermills here, grinding meal for Edinburgh and many nearby villages. The tall Dean Bridge was built by Thomas Telford 1829–31. Kirkbrae House at the southern end was an inn in the 17thC, the Baxter's (Baker's) House of Call. Look at the fine inscribed stone incorporated into the building.

15.00

From Dean Bridge walk along Queensferry Street, soon turning right into Drumsheugh Gardens and Chester Street, then left into Palmerston Place to St Mary's Cathedral, the largest ecclesiastical building in Scotland to be erected since the Reformation. In massive Victorian Gothic style, it was completed in 1917, the result of a bequest by the Walker sisters, who gave their names to the two western towers – Barbara and Mary.

15.45

Now cross West Maitland Street to Morrison Street and walk east to enter the Grassmarket along the West Port, where you will see old Edinburgh tenement buildings in their original state. Granted its charter in 1477, a weekly market was held in the Grassmarket until 1911, and it was the scene of many public executions, including that of the murderer, Burke (of Burke and Hare), who was hanged here in 1829.

16.15

At the top of Candlemaker Row is Greyfriars Kirk, built 1602–20 in the garden of an old monastery. Surrounded by ancient tombs and stones, it is a haven of peace and tranquillity. Have a look at the Covenanters Prison in the churchyard, where the prisoners taken at the Battle of Bothwell Bridge were held, exposed to the elements, for five winter months.

17.00

Outside the church, at the top of Candlemaker Row, is the statue of Edinburgh's most famous 'wee dug', Greyfriars Bobby, whose enduring devotion to his dead master earned him the Freedom of the City, and worldwide fame.

Return to Waverley Station via George IV Bridge, Bank Street and Market Street.

Sightseeing the Easy Way

The Cadies Tour

031–225 6745. Meet outside the Witchery restaurant on Castle Hill for a 75 minute walk, accompanied by a guide costumed as an 18thC Town Guard. *Charge. Advance booking essential.*

Mercat Tours

031–661 4541. Every day at 14.00, starting at the Mercat Cross by St Giles' Cathedral, for a guided walk of the Royal Mile or gallows and graveyards. *Charge. No booking required.*

Robin's Tour

031–557 3443 or 031–661 0125. Starts at the fountain over Waverley market at 11.00, 14.00 *and* 17.00 for a guided walk down the Royal Mile and around the Old Town. *Charge. No booking required.*

New Town Walks

Edinburgh New Town Conservation Centre, 13a Dundas St. 031–557 5222. Explore the First New Town or Calton Hill area. Walks only during *June, July and August, 11.00 and 15.00 Sun.* Also talks on specialised subjects and visits to private houses on *Wed* evenings starting from Register House, Princes St. Advance booking required for evening walks only. *Charge.*

Coach Tours

There is a regular programme of coach tours throughout the year, all leaving from Waverley Bridge. From one hour to a whole day, itineraries include The Grand Tour (a half day exploring the Castle, Royal Mile and Holyrood), The Edinburgh Experience (almost a whole day around the Old Town, Castle and Holyrood), Historic Edinburgh, The Royal Mile and Georgian Edinburgh. Tickets from: **The Ticket Centre**, Waverley Bridge. 031–226 5087 or 031–554 4494. There is also a special Tourist Card, giving the holder unlimited travel on all Lothian Regional Transport services up to 13 days.

Outlook Tower

Castlehill. 031–226 3709. The camera obscura will, on a clear day, project many of the major sights of Edinburgh onto a white concave table, accompanied by an informed commentary. With the Castle and Gladstone's Land close by, it is an excellent introduction to the city, especially if your time is limited. *Open Mon–Sun. Charge.*

Take a Flight

Edinburgh Air Centre, RAF Turnhouse. 031–339 4059/553 6276. Heavily dependent on suitable weather but it is possible to book a light aircraft to fly you over the city, for a spectacular view from the air. *From £10 per person.*

Tourist Guides

The Tourist Information Centre at Waverley Market can supply a list of qualified guides, with a range of 15 languages, who can accompany you, or your group, for half or full day tours, charging between £20.00–£40.00, with a small supplement for languages other than English. **Scottish Tourist Guides Association** 031–661 6038.

Tourist Shuttle Bus

Route 99. A flat-fare circular route encompassing Princes Street, Holyrood, The Royal Mile and the Castle, with unlimited boarding and alighting (so keep your ticket). Open-top buses are used on fine days. Only runs *May–Sep.*

A Day out of Town

Forth Rail Bridge

Those visitors to Edinburgh enjoying the use of a car should take the opportunity of travelling further afield and exploring some of the city's outlying attractions.

The following ideas are in no way intended as a comprehensive list of things to see and do outside the capital. But each itinerary will easily fill a day; if you like to linger then you will have to select only those items that appeal most. Historic buildings, fine scenery, industrial archaeology, museums and boat trips are all well represented. If there is nothing here that suits, or you have an altogether different area in mind, then 20 minutes spent studying a good tourist map before you leave and visits to the helpful local Tourist Information Centres en route will stand you in good stead.

Tourist Information Centres outside Edinburgh

Anstruther Fife
Scottish Fisheries Museum, The Shore. 033–331 0628.
Bannockburn Central
Granada Service Station (M9/M80 junction) 078–681 4111.
Burntisland Fife
4 Kirkgate. 059–287 2667.
Dunbar Lothian
Town House, High Street. 036–863 353.
Dunfermline Fife
East Port 038–372 0999.
Forth Road Bridge Fife
038–341 7759.
Kincardine Bridge Fife
032–483 422.
Kinross Tayside Turfhills
(M90, junction 6). 057–763 680.
Leven Fife
South St. 033–329 464.
Linlithgow Lothian
Burgh Halls, The Cross. 050–684 4600.

Musselburgh Lothian
Brunton Hall. 031–665 6597.
North Berwick Lothian
Quality St. 062–021 97.
St Andrews Fife
South St. 033–472 021.
Stirling Central
Dumbarton Rd. 078–675 019.

Coach tours

For those who do not drive, do not wish to drive, or hire a car, there is a splendid choice of coach trips to places around Edinburgh and further afield. For example, you can take day trips to Loch Lomond, the Fife Coast and St Andrews, the Isle of Arran, the East Lothian Coast, Loch Ness and many other destinations. All coaches leave from Waverley Bridge and the charges are modest. Ask for the timetable and brochure from the **Lothian Regional Transport information desk**, Ticket Centre, Waverley Bridge: 031–226 5087 or 031–554 4494. Services operate *early Apr–Oct.*

Haddington, North Berwick and the Coast

A full day with major sights to see, an exciting boat trip, and plenty of alternative strategies.

Summary of route – eastwards on the A1 to Haddington then – East Linton – Tyninghame – Tantallon – North Berwick and return.

Haddington

The spired **Town House** dominates the main thoroughfare where Court Street divides into Market Street and High Street. It was designed by William Adam, enlarged by Gillespie Graham, and once stood on pillars above an open oat and barley market. You will find a plan of the town here, with all the places of interest marked.

Walk to the left of the Town House along Market Street and on your left you will come to **Mitchell's Close**, a 17thC tenement building restored in 1967 and notable for its stair turret, rubbing board (to protect stone walls from cart wheels) and outside stair. There is a pottery and weavers workshop here. Now walk towards the High Street, cutting through the Vennel, to see the town cross topped with a goat. It dates from 1811 and is the last of a series of earlier crosses. It is unclear why the goat should be the symbol of the town, although it appears also at St Mary's (see below).

Turn left and then right into Sidegate to find **St Ann's Place**, pretty 17thC buildings restored in 1955. Walk on to St Mary's Pleasance, a beautiful 17thC garden of old roses and medicinal herbs to the rear of Alexander Maitland's **Town House**, built in 1680 and now the headquarters of the Lamp of Lothian Collegiate Trust.

You now approach the massive 14thC **Collegiate Church of St Mary**, standing by the River Tyne. Severely damaged during the siege of Haddington 1547–9, the tower, transepts and choir were left roofless for some 400 years. Only the nave survived, preserved by a barrier wall built in 1561 at the instigation of John Knox, who was born in nearby Giffordgate. The final miracle of restoration was achieved 1971–3, when the open parts of the building were re-roofed, and the dividing wall finally removed. The view through the church, the effect of the weathered stone inside, and the ceiling (of fibre-glass) is magnificent. *Open Easter and Apr–Sep 10.00–16.00 Mon–Sat; 13.00–16.00 Sun. Closed Oct–Apr.* The friendly and helpful guides will be happy to show your around, and a short prayer is said daily at 12.00. During the summer there are evening concerts in the church, details from 062–082 3738.

Now rejoin the A1 and drive a further six miles east to East Linton. To the right of the road the massive hump you see is **Traprain Law**, the core of an extinct volcano. It was here in 1919 that a hoard of 4thC Roman silver ware was unearthed which can now be seen in the National Museum of Antiquities in Edinburgh. Turn into the pretty village of East Linton and follow the signs for Preston Mill. You may like to visit the Railway Hotel, (062–086 0298) 5 Bridge St. Ind Coope Burton ale in a friendly local, *open 11.00–23.00 Mon–Sat, 12.00–14.30, 18.00–23.00 Sun.*

Preston Mill

062–086 0426. An astonishingly picturesque working 16thC water mill standing beside a conical red pantiled kiln. It last worked commercially in 1957 and has been fully restored. Owned by the National Trust for Scotland whose representative gives informative guided tours. Take a pleasant stroll across the mill stream to the Phantassie Doocot (dovecot), which gave accommodation for 544 birds – enquire at the mill regarding the key. *Open Apr–Oct 10.00–12.30, 14.00–17.30 Mon–Sat; 14.00–17.30 Sun (Oct closes 16.30); Nov–Mar 10.00–12.30 Sat; 14.00–16.30, 14.00–16.30 Sun. Admission charge.*

Turn right out of Preston Mill to the lovely brown stone village of Tyninghame where you can visit **Tyninghame Gardens**, 062 086 0330, with a 19thC parterre, an 18thC wilderness garden, a walled garden and a secret garden. *Open Jun–Sep 10.30–16.00 Mon–Fri. Admission charge.* Otherwise turn left in the village towards North Berwick. After four miles you will see a sign for Tantallon Castle.

Tantallon Castle
A truly dramatic, theatrical ruin, its tall curtain walls over 4m thick, enclosing a wild headland of unscaleable cliffs. The 14thC stronghold of the Black Douglas family, it was besieged in 1528, and severely damaged in 1651 by General Monck and his Cromwellian army. Climb to the dizzy heights of the ramparts, if you dare, for superb views of the Bass Rock (see below), peer down the freshwater well 33m deep, and explore the gloomy dungeon. When dark storm clouds gather, this is an awesome place. The 17thC dovecot outside the walls holds 1200 nests. *Open Apr–Sep 09.30–19.00 Mon–Sat, 14.00–19.00 Sun; Oct–Mar 09.30–16.00 Mon–Sat, 14.00–16.00 Sun. Admission charge.*

Turn right out of the castle driveway for North Berwick and a boat trip around the Bass Rock or Fidra. If you would rather relax on one of the finest beaches in the area, turn left and look out for the left turn to **Seacliff Beach**. A superb sweep of sand with a miniature harbour and lobster pond cut from living rock at the north end backed by dunes, sea birds, cliffs, wild flowers, shrubs and trees. *Admission charge.*

North Berwick
A robust harbour and lively resort with **Berwick Law**, topped with a Napoleonic watch tower and whalebone arch, to landward. There are boat trips from the harbour in summer to circumnavigate Fidra or the **Bass Rock**, both volcanic cores. The Bass Rock, 7thC retreat of St Baldred, was used as a Covenanters Prison by Charles II and was once held for three years by Jacobite soldiers in the name of the exiled Stuart king after the Battle of Killiecrankie. Robert Louis Stevenson weaved it into his exiting tale of *Catriona*, with David Balfour imprisoned there after the rising of 1745. From the boat you will see gannets diving for fish, comical puffins and the swift angular gliding flight of the fulmar.

Return to Edinburgh along the A194, passing the Nature Reserve at Aberlady Bay and join the main A1, where your day began.

Falkland, St Andrews and the Neuk of Fife

Venturing north across the Forth for a whistle-stop tour of the Kingdom of Fife, a varied and always interesting area often by-passed by those heading for the Highlands.

Summary of route – westwards on the A90 – over the Forth to M90 – A91 to Auchtermuchty then Falkland – Ceres – St Andrews – Crail – Anstruther – Pittenweem – St Monans – Elie and return.

Leave Edinburgh on the A90 following signs for the Forth Road Bridge (toll) and joining the M90 motorway for a swift journey to junction 8, the A91 for St Andrews. The large expanse of water to your right at Kinross is **Loch Leven**, 8 miles around its circumference and noted for its trout fishing. The tower you can see on Castle Island dates from the 14thC. It was here that Mary Queen

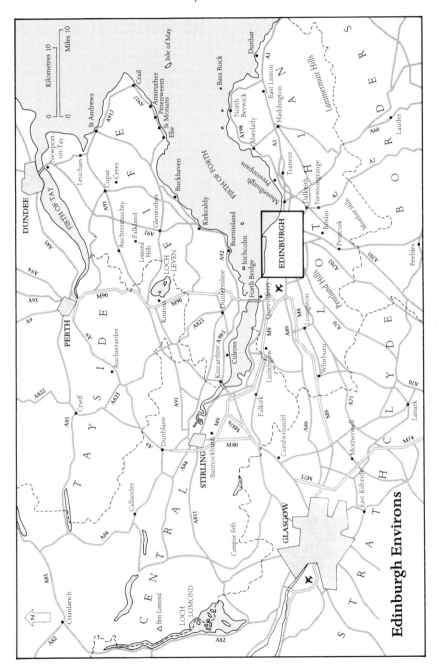

Edinburgh Environs

of Scots was imprisoned after the Battle of Carberry 1567–8. She finally escaped with the help of Willy Douglas, who locked everyone in and threw the keys into the loch. Three hundred years later the keys were retrieved. Follow the A91 to Auchtermuchty, then turn right following signs to Falkland Palace.

Falkland Palace.
031–757 397. In the care of the National Trust for Scotland, but owned by Her Majesty the Queen, Falkland Palace was mainly built between 1501 and 1541 by James IV and James V as a grand hunting lodge amidst the deer and wild boar of the Fife forest, on the site of an earlier 12thC castle.

Informative guides show you the Chapel Royal, the King's Bedchamber where James V is supposed to have died, the Queen's Room, two bedrooms in the gatehouse and the charming and cosy library. The sheltered gardens enclose lawns, shrubs and herbaceous borders, and you can see the oldest Real Tennis court in Britain. It dates from 1539. Admission tickets are purchased at the Town Hall close by and the village, a conservation area since 1970, is rich in period houses and well worth exploring. *Open Apr–Sep 10.00–18.00 Mon–Sat, 14.00–18.00 Sun. Closed Oct Mon–Fri and Nov–Mar. Admission charge* (Scots Guards free!). No dogs.

You may have time before lunch in Ceres to walk on the **Lomond Hills.** The minor road to Leslie (beyond the drinking well, to the left of the violin shop) gives access to a car park and marked trail along the summit ridge, which rises to a height of 522m. The view, on a clear day, is of the whole of Fife and beyond, and will more than repay your efforts.

Now leave Falkland for **Ceres** following the A912, A92 along Stratheden Valley turning sharp right onto the A916

and taking the minor signposted road to Ceres to the left by Hill of Tarvit Mansion House. The black and white Meldrums (031–482 286) is a fine village hotel serving excellent value food and McEwans 80/– ale. Children are welcome, and there is a small garden with swings. *Open 11.00–14.30, 17.00–23.00 Mon–Sat; 12.30–14.30, 18.30–23.00 Sun.* Continue then to the far end of the village for the Fife Folk Museum, or retrace the last mile of your route to Hill of Tarvit.

Fife Folk Museum
The Weigh House, Old High Street. 033–482 380. Housed in a picturesque 17thC group of buildings, this award-winning museum contains a wide range of exhibits illustrating the past life of Fife. Agricultural and medical implements, cobbling, baking, weaving, stonemasonry, costume, toys, ceramics, plus a cottage room setting with box bed, hearth and furnishings, all in the charge of the knowledgeable and enthusiastic curator, Allan Mackay. Note also the old pack-horse bridge across the Ceres Burn and the fine houses and cottages by the Bow Butts (village green). *Open Apr–Nov 14.00–17.00 Mon, Wed–Sat, 14.30–17.30 Sun. Closed Tue. Admission charge.*

Hill of Tarvit
033–453 127. A fine example of an Edwardian mansion house, virtually rebuilt by Sir Robert Lorimer in 1906. French and Chippendale furniture, Flemish tapestries, Chinese porcelain and pictures by Raeburn and Ramsay. Edwardian laundry and potting shed. Pleasant gardens and a fine walk up the hill to the toposcope, for superb views. Owned by the National Trust for Scotland. *Open May–Sep 14.00–17.30 Mon–Sun; Apr & Oct 14.00–17.30 Sat & Sun only. Closed Nov–Mar. Grounds open daily 10.00 to sunset. Admission charge.*

A Day out of Town

Leave behind the Ceres Provost, the jolly 16thC stone figure overlooking the crossroads and take the B939 to St Andrews.

St Andrews

The ancient City of St Andrews was founded by David I in 1140, with the building of the now ruined **Cathedral** starting in 1161. The Cathedral flourished until 1559, when it was destroyed by Reformers, inflamed by John Knox's preaching. Their main targets were the idols and ornaments but the huge building, uncared for, quickly became a ruin. In 1649 Parliament, under Cromwell, took the step of authorising the people of St Andrews to use the Cathedral as a quarry for building stone and many of the stones can be seen built into local houses.

The **Castle** was founded in 1200 as the fortified residence of the Bishop. It is notorious for its fascinating bottle dungeon, cut out of solid rock, from which no one ever escaped. The Castle (033–477 196), Cathedral and Cathedral Museum are *open* 09.30–19.00 *Mon–Sat, 14.00–19.00 Sun; (closes 16.00 Oct–Nov). Museum closed 12.30–13.30. Admission charge to Castle and Museum.*

This is Scotland's oldest university town, where teaching began in 1411. It also claims to be the original home of golf, which is said to have been played here since 1350. Having been banned by Act of Parliament by James II, James III and James IV as a distraction, and played here by Mary Queen of Scots in 1567, St Andrews became the world centre with the formation of the Society of St Andrews Golfers, later to become the **Royal and Ancient Golf Club**. Their clubhouse, built in 1854, is now the world headquarters, open to members only. Visitors can use most of the courses, including the legendary Old Course.

There is a great deal to see and do in the seaside town of St Andrews, but to complete this tour you must take the A917 signposted to Crail, to visit the picturesque fishing villages of the Neuk of Fife. Depending on your schedule, you may not be able to visit them all. Crail and St Monans are outstanding.

Crail

Of remarkable picture postcard prettiness, Crail has been in the fish business since the 9thC, when salt herring was exported to the Continent. Its Royal Charter was granted by Robert the Bruce in 1310, and included the right to trade on a Sunday. This explains why John Knox chose to preach a particularly forthright sermon from the 12thC church of St Mary's. As well as the superb harbour (still a working fishing port) there is a new local museum in Marketgate.

Now just follow the A917 in a south westerly direction.

Anstruther

The locals call this 'Anster' – it was at one time Scotland's major herring port, until the silver darlings deserted these waters. Now it's the tourists who provide the mainstay of the local economy. Boats fish for crab, lobster and prawn, and take out parties of fishermen, sightseers and divers, often to the Isle of May, some five miles offshore.

At the north end of Shore Street is the **Scottish Fisheries Museum**, in St Ayles Land (033–331 0628), a property site which dates from 1318. The buildings were themselves net lofts and fishermen's stores, and the collection of artefacts, pictures and models, together with a small aquarium, is fascinating. *Open Apr–Oct 10.00–17.30 Mon–Sat, 14.00–17.00 Sun; Nov–Mar 14.00–17.00 Mon–Fri & Sun, 10.00–17.00 Sat. Admission charge.* If you have the time or inclination, the

Sun pub, (033–331 0068) right next door, is recommended. McEwans ales and tasty snacks in simple unspoilt surroundings. *Open 11.00–24.00 Mon–Sat; 12.00–14.30, 18.30–23.00 Sun.*

Pittenweem

This is now the premier fishing port on the East Neuk, maintaining an active fishing fleet, and giving the harbour a business-like air. The town grew around the 12thC Priory, and some later 16thC parts of the buildings can be seen.

St Monans

A small harbour dominated by the paraphernalia of a long-established boat-builders and hemmed in by close terraces of old houses and cottages.

Several of the old houses in the harbour have been restored by the National Trust. The real joy here is the church to the south of the village, where the graveyard adjoins the rocky shore. The original building certainly dates from at least 1362. The church was dramatically restored in the reign of James III. The unusual T-plan results from the fact the nave was never built. Its chunky tower and squat steeple stand four square against the south east winds, which can drench the old gravestones with spray. The white painted interior is light and refreshing, with a fine model ship hanging from the ceiling, and reminders of its seafaring connections all around.

Elie

A wide open harbour popular with windsurfers and sailors, who relax and discuss their exploits over a pint of Belhaven ale in the superb wood-panelled Ship Inn (033–333 0246), by the shore. *Open 11.00–24.00 Mon–Sat; 12.30–14.30, 18.30–23.00 Sun.*

Now return to Edinburgh by the coast road, through Buckhaven, Kirkcaldy and Burntisland.

Culross, Bannockburn and Linlithgow Palace

This day trip delves deeply into Scottish history, beginning at the preserved village of Culross, on the shores of the Forth, then on to Stirling via the scene of the Battle of Bannockburn, and returning via the brooding Linlithgow Palace. There is also the chance of a boat trip for weekend travellers.

Summary of route – leave Edinburgh on the A90 west, cross the Forth Bridge, turn left onto the A985 through Rosyth then Culross – Kincardine Bridge – Bannockburn – Stirling – Linlithgow and return.

Culross

038–388 0359. Clearly signposted off the A985, 12 miles west of the Forth Road Bridge. A working village with shops and pubs, where the residents are totally accustomed to the regular influx of visitors.

In a very poor state of repair by the 1930s, this was one of the National Trust for Scotland's first rescue enterprises, and the result is the fine array of 16thC and 17thC buildings we see today. Indeed such was the care exercised that the electricity sub-station was installed inside one of the cottages, and television aerials, gas pipes and telephone wires are all discreetly hidden away. The settlement here was founded by St Serf who on landing, called it Culenros, meaning 'holly point'. His remains were worshipped here during the Middle Ages, and eventually the **Abbey** was founded in 1217, on land given by the Earl of Fife. The Cistercian monks, who came from Kinloss, were both expert sheep-farmers and miners, exploiting the rich coal seam which lies just below the surface. Gradually the settlement grew, until in 1490 it was created a Burgh of

94

Barony. William Colville, a lay administrator, saw the Abbey through the turbulent period of the Reformation, eventually overseeing the dissolution of the monastery and transferring the revenues to his family, who became very wealthy as a result. In 1604 Sir James Colville was made Lord Colville of Culross.

The town continued to prosper, thanks to the coal deposits and the expertise of a local man, George Bruce, whose efficient extraction methods resulted in there being a surplus for export. At this time the mine stretched out under the waters of the Forth, with a shaft called the Moat Pit, built up from below the low water mark. Ships were loaded directly from here, thus avoiding harbour dues. This curiosity was visited in 1617 by King James VI, eight years before it was destroyed by exceptionally high tides and gales. However, mining continued from pits on land, and this, together with salt extraction and the making of iron girdles, ensured prosperity through the 16th, 17th and 18th centuries.

The inevitable steady decline came with the beginning of the Industrial Revolution. The population was forced to find other means to survive – mainly fishing and farming – but the days when ships from the low countries crowded the harbour had gone. In the 1780s, the poor receiving aid from the church numbered over 60.

Begin your walk around Culross at the **Town House**, built in 1626 and where the Trust's informative audio visual presentations are given. Then explore the **Palace**, George Bruce's fine house, with a rare decorative interior, built between 1597 and 1611, before wandering along to the Mercat (or market) Cross and, if you feel energetic, up to the remains of the Abbey. All the while, there are fine views of the Forth between white harled walls and over

the warm orange pantiled roofs. Town House 038–388 0359, *open May–Sep 10.00–13.00, 14.00–17.00 Mon–Fri, 14.00–17.00 Sat & Sun. Closed Oct–Apr. Admission charge for audio-visual presentation.* Palace (038–388 0608) *open Apr–Sep 09.30–19.00 Mon–Sat, 14.00–19.00 Sun; Oct–Mar 09.30–12.30, 13.30–16.00 Mon–Sat, 14.00–16.00 Sun. Admission charge.*

Continue west on the minor road through Culross, passing Blair Castle and on to cross the Kincardine Bridge.

Kincardine Bridge
Opened in 1936 this was the major road bridge crossing of the tidal Forth until the completion of the suspension bridge in 1964. As you approach from Culross you can clearly see the middle section which swings open on a central pivot to let ships through. It doesn't operate as frequently as it used to, but it is still in perfect working order – the mechanism is so smooth that a 10p coin balanced on edge in the control room above the pivot will not topple over during operation.

Continue across the bridge to pick up the M9 motorway to Stirling. After 7 miles you will see the Bannockburn Heritage Centre signposted at junction 9, 2 miles before Stirling. Follow signs to the Centre.

Bannockburn Heritage Centre
078–681 2664. An excellent and dramatic audio visual presentation clearly explains the events leading up to Robert the Bruce's victory over the English forces of King Edward II in June 1314, thus regaining independence for Scotland. There is also an excellent book and souvenir shop. Then walk beyond the car park to the site of the battle, marked by the rotunda and the statue of Bruce, which was inaugurated by Queen Elizabeth II in 1964. The 58 acres of grassland give fine views over the Ban

nock Burn, and Stirling Castle away in the distance. *Open Apr–Oct 10.00–18.00 Mon–Sun. Admission charge for audio visual.* No charge to site of battle.

Turn left out of the Bannockburn Heritage Centre and follow signs for the centre of Stirling, then signs for the Castle. Drive right up to the car park on the Castle forecourt.

Stirling Castle
078–650 000. Strikingly similar to Edinburgh Castle, both in style and situation, this great castle would be worthy of a visit just for the views alone, its fairytale position on the summit of a high craggy hill giving an unequalled vista over the surrounding land.

Its strategic importance was once greater than that of Edinburgh, since it commanded the crossing of the Forth and stood at the very heart of the nation. At the time of the Battle of Bannockburn the fortress would have been timber built – what we see today dates from the 15thC and owes its existence to King James III, whose fine Gothic Great Hall, turreted gatehouse and curtain walls form the core of the complex. Further additions and numerous depredations have taken place since then, especially towards the end of the 18thC, when the Great Hall was ruthlessly converted into a barracks.

On 9 September 1543 the infant Mary Queen of Scots was crowned here, the start of a story which no historical novelist could better, and which ended so tragically at Fotheringhay in 1587. A reminder of its function as a palace lies outside the walls but is best seen from the ramparts on the west side – the mounds and ramps of a vast ornamental knot garden, the last visible remains of the King's Park. The last military action here took place during the unsuccessful Jacobite rebellion of 1745, when the Bonnie Prince laid siege to the castle

garrison under General Blakeney, was repulsed with heavy losses and finally retreated in the face of a force commanded by the Duke of Cumberland. Even though it was usurped as a castle and a palace by Edinburgh and Holyrood, Stirling's .place in Scottish history will remain. It is now the headquarters of the Argyll and Sutherland Highlanders, who maintain a museum within the walls. Bookshop, café and audio visual. *Open Jun–Aug 10.00–20.00 Mon–Sat, 11.00–20.00 Sun; Apr, May & Sep 10.00–18.45 Mon–Sat, 11.00–18.00 Sun; Oct–Mar 10.00–16.00 Mon–Sat, 13.00–16.00 Sun. Admission charge.*

The town of Stirling grew around the castle, and many 16th, 17th and 18thC buildings survive. It had the distinction of becoming Scotland's youngest university town, when a new centre of learning was opened in 1967, built around a loch and the excellent MacRobert Arts Centre. Tea shops, pubs and restaurants will be found in plenty, should you require refreshment. To the north east, and visible from the castle and miles around, is the **Wallace Monument**, commemorating Sir William Wallace's victory over the English at the Battle of Stirling Bridge on 11 September 1297. The monument itself was built 1861–9, with the statue being added in 1887.

Now retrace your route past Bannockburn and back to the motorway, heading in the direction of Edinburgh. Turn off at junction 4 towards the coast and follow signs for Linlithgow Palace, which is behind the Tourist Information Centre in the main street.

Linlithgow Palace
031–244 3101. A wonderful, brooding, roofless shell standing by a loch, built over a 100 year period from 1425 by the Stuart kings and Mary Queen of Scots was born here in December 1542. This

magnificent royal palace fell into disrepair after the Union of the Crowns in 1603, when the Scottish Court moved south to London. Part of the roof fell in and, in spite of repair work, the last king to stay here was Charles I in 1633. It was gutted by fire when occupied by the Duke of Cumberland during the '45 rebellion. The Church of St Michael was built concurrently with the Palace – it was here that James IV saw the ghost which warned him of defeat at Flodden Field. The aluminium pseudo-spire, added in 1964, is a poor substitute for the original open stone crown. *Open Apr–Sep 09.30–19.00 Mon–Sat, 14.00–19.00 Sun; Oct–Mar 09.30–16.00 Mon–Sat, 14.00–16.00 Sun. Admission charge.*

Canal Museum

Canal Basin, Linlithgow. On the Union Canal, which joined the Forth and Clyde Canal at Falkirk to link the great cities of Glasgow and Edinburgh. It last saw commercial use in 1933 but recent interest in restoration has made this stretch navigable, and trips can be had in the *Victoria*, a fine replica of a Victorian steam packet boat. The museum is open, and trips are run, from *Easter–Sep 14.00–17.00 Sat & Sun only. Museum admission free, charge for boat trips.*

Now follow the signs for the M9 motorway and return to Edinburgh.

Hopetoun House, Queensferry and a trip down the Forth

The essence of this day out is the sharp contrast between one of Scotland's most sumptuous stately homes and the austerity of life on an island abbey. There is also a chance to explore Queensferry, another of Edinburgh's villages.

Summary of route – leave Edinburgh

on the A90 west, turn off for Queensferry just before the Forth Bridge. Hopetoun House is signposted to the west, Hawes Pier for the trip to the island is under the railway bridge. Make sure you arrive at Hopetoun House as soon as it opens, and check times of boat trip before you start out.

Hopetoun House

031–331 2451. A superb Adam mansion standing in 100 acres of parkland bordering the Forth, this has been the home of the Hope family since building began in 1699. The present occupant is the 3rd Marquess of Linlithgow, who occupies part of the building as a tenant of the charitable trust established in 1974 to own and preserve this unique building and its contents.

The original building was designed by Sir William Bruce, but it was greatly altered and enlarged by William Adam in 1721, and work continued under the direction of his three sons after his death in 1748. Most of the furnishings and furniture that you will see are original, and date from this period.

A surprisingly modest doorway brings you into the bright, sparkling **entrance hall**, decorated with Italian marble reliefs brought to Scotland in 1720 by the second Marquess of Annandale. There is also a fine white marble fireplace dating from 1755.

The **libraries** are altogether more homely, note the fine books available to leaf through – including one detailing the building of the Forth Rail Bridge – and the intriguing French slate mantle clock with perpetual calendar and phases of the moon. The comfortable wood panelled **garden parlour** looks out over the lawns, and once served as the main entrance from the gardens. Brightly decorated in rich crimson and white, with wall paintings by James Norie circa 1750, the **Bruce bedchamber** contains a gilt four poster bed supplied by Mathias Lock of London in 1768. Intricate carvings by Alexander Eizat decorate the curving stairway to the upper floor. The murals here were painted as recently as 1967 by the Scottish artist William McLaren, commissioned by Lord Linlithgow as a tribute to his first wife, who died in 1963. The whole stairway is lit by a glass dome.

The **west Wainscot rooms**, sumptuously decorated with Dutch tapestries and japanned furniture circa 1680 represent the work of Bruce, and have survived unaltered.

The walls of the **yellow drawing room** were covered in silk brocade around 1850, and complement the exquisite gilded ceiling by John Dawson. Furniture is by James Cullen, a contemporary of Chippendale, and the window and door frames are by John Paterson, the estate joiner. This room is part of the suite of State Apartments, and it was here that Sir Henry Raeburn, portrait painter, and Sir Adam Ferguson, keeper of the Regalia in Scotland, were knighted by King George IV on 29 August 1822, as part of his state visit to Scotland.

The **red drawing room**, another of the State Apartments, is decorated with red silk damask dating from 1766. Furniture is arranged 'parade style', leaving the floor space clear for entertaining, the room's main function. John Dawson's gilded plaster-work ceiling is a magnificent example of the craft, and one of the finest in existence. The chimney piece, with its voluptuous marble ladies, was made by Michael Rysbrack in 1756. In its entirety the room is a wonderfully preserved demonstration of the genius of the Adams.

The **state dining room**, created in 1820 by the fourth Earl of Hopetoun, has retained all its Regency decoration and furnishings, including such items as the Derby dessert service and wine cool-

ers. Note the leather-like gold wall covering and family portraits. The adjoining serving room stands above the kitchen – the food arrived by steam heated railway! The brass servants' bells were brought here from the basement hall.

A stairway leads to the small family **museum** and the rooftop **observatory**, which gives an excellent view of the Forth, its bridges and its islands. Situated in the South Pavilion and entered from the forecourt, the **ballroom**, originally designed as the library and once used as an indoor riding school, now displays a set of late 17thC French tapestries illustrating scenes from Virgil's *Aeneid*.

The grounds are particularly pleasant where they border the foreshore and the red deer park. A nature trail can be followed which leads down to the water's edge, once an oyster bed rich enough to supply the house. St Kilda sheep are kept by the main driveway, there is a museum in the stables and walled gardens to the south. Restaurant, tea room, shop and picnic area. *Open Easter and May–Sep 11.00–17.30 Mon–Sun. Closed Oct–Apr. Admission charge.*

Now head back towards Queensferry, drive through the village on the coast road to the Hawes Pier under the Forth Railway Bridge.

Forth Railway Bridge

Thomas Bouch was to have built the railway bridge across the Forth. But when his Tay Bridge collapsed so disastrously in the storm of December 1879, with the loss of 90 lives, there was an understandable reluctance to trust his designs, and the task was given instead to Sir John Fowler and Benjamin Baker. With the Tay disaster still fresh in their minds, they built this massive all steel bridge comprising three double cantilevers, over one and a half miles long in total (there is 1m difference in its length between mid-summer and mid-winter) and giving a clearance of 110m under the two main spans. A graceful cobweb seen from afar, the enormity of its construction can only be appreciated close to. This tribute to Victorian engineering skill was built between 1882–90 and 7000 gallons of paint are needed to cover its surface area of over 135 acres. Modern paint technology obviates the need for the once notorious continual painting, although at the time of writing (May 1987) it looked in need of attention. Incredibly it survived World War II undamaged.

Forth Road Bridge
No less significant than the rail bridge, since it obviated the use of the infamous ferries which had existed here since 1129. They caused no end of delays during the summer holiday period with long queues of traffic waiting on both banks. This elegant suspension bridge was opened in 1964. The largest in Europe when built, it cost £20 million and took six years to construct.

Hawes Pier
The trip boat to Inchcolm leaves from this jetty, built by John Rennie in 1812.

Maid of the Forth
031–331 1454. 100 seater trip boat with an observation deck, heated saloon and bar. The friendly crew gives an informative commentary on the 2½ hour round trip to Inchcolm. Usual trip times are May–Jun & Sep 14.00 Sat & Sun; Jul & Aug Mon–Sun but always ring and check times and availability (especially in rough weather). Ticket office on Hawes Pier opens one hour before boat leaves. Wear warm, windproof clothing on all but the warmest days.

Inchcolm
The Iona of the east, lying less than a

mile off the Fife coast, was occupied by hermits throughout the Dark Ages and a primitive cell, although much altered, still exists. Indeed it was the shelter offered here to the storm-bound King Alexander I in 1123 which led to the King's vow to found a monastery on the island, dedicated to St Colm.

Building began the following year, and in 1162 it is known to have been occupied by Augustinian canons. Administered by successive bishops of Dunkeld, the community quickly established itself in the religious life of the country; regarded as a shrine to St Columba, it became an important religious site. The bell tower was built and the chancel enlarged during the 13thC, with the remains of the three bishops of Dunkeld being transferred here from the abbey church. Part of one of these tombs has survived, and its painted decoration can be clearly seen. Bishop Richard of Inverkeithing had his heart interned in the north wall upon his death in 1272, and a new north transept and chapter-house were added.

The Wars of Independence, which began at the end of the 13thC and continued on and off for another 300 years, brought with them a new austerity and ultimately the ruin of the Abbey. The English raided and plundered, and the plague also took its toll.

A period of relative tranquility at the start of the 16thC came to an end with another English attack in 1542 – following this the Abbey fell into the hands of Sir James Stewart of Beath. Religious life on the island, with its solemn mass conducted for centuries, came to an end by 1560. The abbey lands became part of a lordship, confirmed by Act of Parliament in 1611.

Used as a quarantine station for plague stricken ships, a hospital, and fortified during the Napoleonic and First World wars, the ruins were eventually taken into government care and are now held in trust by the Secretary of State for Scotland. Hunter and Rae Brown now live on the island all year round as custodians, keeping the grounds and the gardens immaculate. The abbey buildings are worthy of exploration – notable are the **warming room**, the only place where the canons kept a fire, a 13thC octagonal **chapter house** and the view from the top of the tower. Be warned, however, this involves climbing a very narrow and steep circular stone stairway, followed by an exposed wooden stair to a precarious position behind a low wall. There are crescents of sand either side of the abbey, and excellent walks around the island, which is a nature reserve, populated with seabirds and seals. The island is *open every day of the year, except Sun morning*. A landing fee is charged, although this is already paid if you come on the *Maid of the Forth*. If you would like to spend longer on the island, there is a ferry service from Aberdour in Fife, mornings by arrangement, then 13.30, 14.30 and 15.30 *every day mid-Jun to early Sep; May, early Jun and late Sep Sat & Sun only or by arrangement*. All dependent on weather and tides. Contact Dougal Barrie, Hawkcraig House, 038–386 0335.

Queensferry
Known as South Queensferry to distinguish it from its counterpart on the north bank, this village at the foot of a steep hill by the Forth has managed to retain its identity in spite of the development which surrounds it. The Romans crossed the Forth here, and a ferry was operated by Carmelite Friars from the nearby monastery, but the service did not become formally established until 1129 during the reign of King David I. It was used before then, however, by Queen Margaret, wife of Malcolm Canmore who journeyed regularly between Edin-

burgh Castle and the Palace at Dunfermline. Graduating from oars to sail and finally to diesel powered car ferries, what was probably one of the most ancient ferry crossings in the world came to an end with the opening of the Forth Road Bridge in 1964. A relief for Edinburgh folk who suffered long delays during holiday periods, but which the passage of time has tinged with a certain regret.

The ferry and the 17thC Hawes Inn (031–331 1990) were featured in Robert Louis Stevenson's *Kidnapped*. Arrols ale, food, children's room. *Open* 11.00–23.00 *Mon–Sat*, 12.30–23.00 *Sun*. The oldest surviving house, the **Black Castle**, dates from 1626 and stands in East Terrace next to the Forth Bridge Hotel, with its fine sign. Also look at the **Tolbooth**, remodelled in 1720, it has an external staircase and pointed steeple. It was built as a prison. Bright and breezy, and popular with windsurfers and dinghy sailors, Queensferry is well worth visiting in its own right. From here you can walk by the shore to Cramond, four miles to the east. Should your trip to Inchcolm have to be abandoned due to the weather, or if you have an aversion to boats or ruined abbeys, you should consider a visit to Dalmeny House, east of Queensferry.

Dalmeny House
Queensferry. 031–331 1888. The home of the 7th Earl and Countess of Rosebery, whose family has lived at Dalmeny, by the shore of the Forth, for over 300 years. The present house dates from 1815 and was the first Tudor Gothic Revival house in Scotland, designed by William Wilkins. The richly decorated exterior and the splendid hammerbeam and fan vaulted roofs are particularly notable. The Rosebery Collection includes paintings by Gainsborough, Raeburn and Reynolds, Goya tapestries

and 17thC furniture. In addition the Rothschild Collection, which came into the family in 1878, comprises French 18thC furniture, and porcelain. In the Napoleon Room you will see furniture used by him when his power was greatest, plus the simple desk and chairs used during his exile on St Helena. The sheltered garden contains many rhododendrons and azaleas. Teas. *Open May–Sep 14.00–17.30 Sun–Thur. Closed Oct–Mar. Admission charge.*

Butterflies, Mining Museum and Rosslyn Chapel

An excellent trip for a bad weather day, since these attractions are all under cover. Again contrasts abound – tropical butterflies, life in a 19thC coal mining village and some unique 15thC architecture.

Summary of route – leave Edinburgh south east on the A7. The Butterfly Farm is on the right about one mile before Eskbank – then A7 to Newtongrange – B704, A6094 to Rosewell – B7003 to Roslin and return.

Edinburgh Butterfly Farm
On A7 north west of Dalkeith. 031–663 4932. An opportunity to see hundreds of butterflies and some tropical birds in a warm, humid indoor jungle landscaped with pools and waterfalls. Some species, such as the Atlas moth, have a wingspan of 140mm or more, and are quite likely to settle on your head. It is sobering to reflect that our own countryside once supported a rich variety of lepidoptera. Farms such as this, as well as being extremely enjoyable, provide valuable research information which may one day contribute towards reintroductions. Other exhibits show tarantulas, wood ant colonies and the

inside workings of a bee hive. There is an adventure playground, tea room and large garden centre adjoining. *Open Apr–Oct 10.00–17.00 Mon–Sun. Admission charge.*

Now turn right onto the A7 through Eskbank (Dalkeith) to Newtongrange.

Scottish Mining Museum
Lady Victoria Colliery, Newtongrange. 031–663 7519. Work on sinking the shaft here began in 1890 and took the Lothian Coal Company four years to complete. With a depth of 503m it was at the time the deepest in Scotland, 6m in diameter and brick lined throughout. The massive winding machinery, which you will see in operation and for which you will have to wear a bright red safety helmet, was powered by a 2400 horsepower engine with twin cylinders over 1m across pushing pistons with a 2m stroke. It was built in Kilmarnock by Grant, Ritchie & Co, and could raise either 8 tons of coal or 30 men with each lift. Steam was provided by 12 hand-stoked Lancashire boilers and the whole system worked successfully, apart from a fire in the wood lined engine house in 1906, and without loss of life until the colliery closed in 1982. On your tour of the colliery you will also see a simulation of unloading the cage, with plenty of clanging and banging, and heaving of tubs.

But perhaps the highlight of the museum is the evocative presentation of mining life in Newtongrange in the early 20thC, recreated in a series of tableaux, complete with sounds and smells, upstairs in the former company offices. Beginning with the fictional Willie Drysdale leaving for work early in the morning, it takes us through life in the colliery; Lord and Lady Lothian in conversation and Willie's interview with Mungo Mackay, Agent, General Manager, strict disciplinarian and all-powerful ruler of the mine and the village. We also see Willie's hard pressed and very pregnant wife, and finish with him disappearing into the Dean Tavern.

The coal company housed its workers in sound single storey cottages, creating the largest pit village in Scotland, and catered for social, physical and spiritual needs with bowling greens, a Co-op and churches. Shop, teas and licensed restaurant. Mining Museum *open 10.00–17.00 Tue–Fri, 12.00–17.00 Sat & Sun. The winding gear operates every hour on the hour until 16.00. Admission charge.*

From Newtongrange, continue south on the A7 for half a mile, then turn right on the B704 for Bonnyrigg. Turn left on the A6094 to Rosewell. Turn right in village to Roslin. Follow signs to Rosslyn Chapel.

Rosslyn Chapel
031–440 2159. Begun in 1446 and completed some 40 years later, this magnificent chapel was founded by Sir William St Clair, third (and last) Prince of Orkney, and man of great intellect. It was planned as one arm of a cross-shaped sanctuary, with a tower in the centre, to be the Collegiate Church of St Matthew; about 30 such churches, with schools attached, were built around this time as spiritual centres and seats of learning. The rest of the building was, however, not completed, due to Sir William's death in 1484.

The outside walls of the chapel are strengthened by large stone buttresses topped with ornamented pinnacles, from which rise flying buttresses, to stabilise the roof-bearing walls. On entering, one is literally stunned by the richness of the carving, which was executed by the best local masons and sculptors augmented by craftsmen from France, Italy, Spain and Portugal. Although foreign influence is apparent, the character of the whole interior remains essentially Scottish. The feature for which this beautiful building is best known is the Apprentice Pillar, intricately decorated, finely sculptured, and now part of legend. For it seems that the master mason, asked to carry out the work, felt he should visit Europe, Rome especially, to study the carving there before completing what would surely be his masterpiece at Rosslyn. But while he was away, his apprentice dreamed that he should do the work, and in the absence of the master mason this is what he did. When the master returned, his anger was such that he killed the apprentice with his mallet, within the church. True or not, it is known that the building was re-consecrated by the Bishop of St Andrews around this time.

The chapel is entered via the charming gift shop, heavy with the scent of pot-pourri, dried flowers, honey and cakes, an excellent place for tea. *Open 10.00–17.00 Mon–Sat, 12.00–16.45 Sun. Admission charge.*

The chapel, and the now ruined **Rosslyn Castle** both stand in the wooded valley of the River Esk. The Castle can only be approached by a bridge, formerly a draw bridge. Immediately through the ancient archway may be seen the Lantern or Lamp Tower built in 1304 by the first Earl of Orkney. The Castle was devastated when Henry VIII sent the Earl of Hertford to Scotland to burn Edinburgh, Craigmillar, Jedburgh, Melrose and Rosslyn castles, but the chapel escaped. The area was much loved by William and Dorothy Wordsworth, and Sir Walter Scott, who came to live in nearby Lasswade with his new wife Charlotte Margaret Carpenter in 1798. The Wordsworths visited him there while staying at the inn in Roslin.

As you enter the village you'll see footpaths and a nature trail signposted. Now drive through the village, following the minor road, then turn right onto the A703 to return to Edinburgh.

Pubs

The great advantage of Edinburgh, and indeed Scotland as a whole, has been the enlightened approach to licensing hours in the pubs, confirming once again that Scots' law is well in advance of English! Individual pubs can easily obtain a licence to stay open all day. Many of the best pubs are situated close together in the centre of town, making Edinburgh a perfect place for an all-day pub crawl. There is also a good selection of pubs outside Edinburgh.

Edinburgh first established a Society of Brewers in 1596 and once supported 36 independent breweries. Unfortunately many of the pubs have now fallen under the shadow of the large corporations, who impose a restricted choice of ales and theme decor. But this is not to say that variety and vibrancy can no longer be found in Edinburgh pubs. There are the architectural delights of Bennets Bar and the Guildford Arms; the cellar-like Bannerman's; the suave and demure Kay's; the earthy friendliness of Clarkes; The Old Chain Pier looking over the Forth and The Shore by the harbour at Leith; and the almost legendary beer and service at the Athletic Arms (also known as the Gravediggers).

Once inside, the traditional pub beverage is, of course, beer and all the places recommended serve real ale. Real ale, as opposed to keg, is unpasteurised and uncarbonated but if you prefer keg, most pubs serve it as well. Remember when ordering your ale at the bar that heavy is stronger than light, but light is darker in colour, and 80/– (eighty shilling) is stronger than 60/– (sixty shilling). A possible area of confusion for the uninitiated is the peculiarly Scottish tall fount. North of the border the preference is for ale to be dispensed under considerable pressure using the tall fount to give the ale a creamy texture and a full head. In its true form it's an excellent way of serving real ale.

If your taste is for something stronger, then of course you must try Scotch whisky, either a blend, made from malt and grain, or preferably one of the many single malts, each the product of one distillery only, and each with its own subtle flavour. And in the land of 'uisge-beagh', the water of life, please show your respect by asking for it by brand, never just whisky or 'scotch'.

The following pubs and bars are recommended for atmosphere, meeting places, a good pint of real ale, or for being close to places of interest.

Abbotsford E3
Rose St. 031–225 5276. A comfortable and traditional Edinburgh institution close to the city's financial centre. Wood panelling and leather benches surround a richly carved central bar. Broughton Greenmantle is served, and there is excellent lunchtime food. *Open 12.00–14.15, 18.30–22.00 Mon–Sat. Closed Sun.*

Athletic Arms (Gravediggers)
11–13 Angle Park Terrace (about 1 mile south west of the West End). 031–225 5276. The beer in this bright, basic, busy pub is claimed to be the best kept in Edinburgh. It's McEwans 80/–, and when Hearts are playing at home, or there is a match at Murrayfield, the consumption is awesome. Service is always excellent, from an array of tall red founts. When it is packed decide how many pints you want, hold up a similar number of fingers, then set about getting to the bar to collect. Dalry cemetery is right opposite – hence the nickname. *Open 11.00–14.30, 17.00–22.30 Mon–Sun.*

Auld Worthies
178–182 Dalry Rd. 031–337 5722. A fine, wood-panelled old local with leaded glass windows and an open fire. McEwans 80/– and Younger's No 3 is dispensed by air pressure from tall founts. The juke box and television can intrude. *Open 11.00–24.00 Mon–Sat; 12.30–14.30, 18.30–23.00 Sun.*

Baillie B1
2 St Stephen St, Stockbridge. 031–225 4673. Very dark, triangular, wood-panelled bar on the corner with N.W. Circus Place, under a musical instrument and vacuum cleaner shop. Belhaven 80/–, McEwan's 70/– and 80/– and Younger's No 3 are all available, and lunches are served. St Stephen Street is an excellent area for a browse around the shops. *Open 11.00–24.00 Mon–Sat; 12.30–14.30, 18.30–23.00 Sun.*

Bannerman's Bar F5
212 Cowgate, tucked into the shadow of South Bridge. 031–556 3254. Flag floors, stone walls, barrel-vault ceilings, wooden benches and pews – as well as an absence of recorded music – make this pub excellent for an intimate chat. There is a good choice of ale, including Lorimer & Clarks and Arrol's, and food is served all day. Well worth the short detour if you are walking the Royal Mile, since the choice in the High Street is lamentable. Live folk music on Mon, Tue, Wed and Sun. *Open 11.00–24.00 Mon–Sat; 12.30–14.30, 18.00–23.00 Sun.*

Beehive (Drones) D5
18–20 Grassmarket. 031–225 7171. There is McEwan's 70/– and 80/– served by air pressure here. The dimly lit bar is decorated in a comfortable style, with settles, and prints of old Edinburgh on the walls. Bar meals are served, and there is

a smart, international restaurant adjoining. Open 11.00–23.00 Mon–Sat; 18.30–23.00 Sun.

Bennets Bar C7
8 Leven St. 031–229 6850. It is worth every step of the walk along Lothian Road to visit this Edwardian gem. Admire the leaded glass windows, then walk into a miniature palace of mahogany mirrors, art nouveau glass, cherubs, and a richly decorated ceiling. Make yourself comfortable on leather seats and enjoy the intricacies of the bar and counter, where you can order McEwans 70/- and 80/-, served from tall founts, of course. They also have their own brand of whisky available. Lunchtime food (not Sun). Open 11.00–24.00 Mon–Sat; 12.30–14.30, 18.30–23.00 Sun.

Blue Blazer C5
2 Spittal St. 031–229 5030. A comfortable pub, richly decorated with brewing ephemera and handy for the Usher Hall. McEwan's 70/- and 80/- is served by air pressure from tall founts. Open 11.00–23.00 Mon & Tue, 11.30–23.30 Wed–Sat, 12.30–14.30 Sun.

Bull and Bush C5
81–83 Lothian Rd. 031–229 4395. Just across the road from the Usher Hall, so ideal for a pre or post-concert pint. It is large and fairly opulent, and Tennent Heriot 80/- is served. Bar meals. Open 11.00–23.30 Mon–Wed; 11.00–24.00 Thur; 11.00–01.00 Fri & Sat; 12.30–14.30, 18.30–23.00 Sun.

Café Royal Circle Bar F2
West Register St. 031–556 1884. A stylish, upmarket Victorian exhibition bar, with plenty of marble, brass and walnut, and tiled portraits of Victorian industrial heroes by Doulton on the walls. The atmosphere, usually quiet and chatty, can get livelier when the right crowd

comes in. There is good bar food, and an oyster bar adjoining. Tall founts dispense McEwan's 70/- and Younger's No 3 to quench your thirst. Open 11.00–23.00 Mon–Thur; 11.00–24.00 Fri & Sat; 19.00–23.00 Sun.

Cavern
7 Bernard St, Leith. 031–554 7515. Licensed for the benefit of the dockers, so the day starts here at 06.00. The single bar is smart and well kept, and gleaming brass tall founts continually dispense McEwan's 80/- by air pressure. The bar food, available lunchtime and evenings, is good and reasonably priced. Open 06.00–23.00 Mon–Sat; 12.30–14.00, 18.30–23.00 Sun.

Clark's Bar
142 Dundas St. 031–556 1067. A really good, unpretentious, friendly Edinburgh boozer, full of locals being served McEwan's 80/- by cheerful staff. If you prefer to sit, there are a couple of rooms with chairs and tables at the back. Snacks available. Open 11.00–22.30 Mon–Wed; 11.00–23.00 Thur–Sat; 12.30–14.30, 18.30–23.00 Sun.

Coppers F4
19 Cockburn St. 031–225 1441. A bright, lively and friendly one room local with a good choice of well kept ale – Lorimer and Clark's 70/- and 80/- and Arrol's 70/- are recommended. Good bar food. Open 12.00–23.00 Mon–Wed; 12.00–24.00 Thur–Sat; 12.30–14.30, 18.30–23.00 Sun.

Cramond Brig
Queensferry Rd (A90), on the way into Edinburgh from the Forth Bridge. 031–339 4350. There is McEwan's 80/- for Dad, who can safely bring the rest of the family here and join them in a nice room set aside. Excellent food is served all day, and the historic bridge is close by. You can read all about it on page 76,

Pubs

in the Village Edinburgh section. Cramond village is about one mile to the north of here – turn left along Whitehouse Road at the Barnton Hotel (McEwan's 80/- and also worth a visit). Open 11.00–23.00 Mon–Sat; 12.30–23.00 Sun.

Cramond Inn
Cramond Glebe Rd. 031–336 2035. A white painted fisherman's pub, dating from 1670, which has moved up-market in line with the village of the same name. Admire the quayside cottages, the church and the Roman remains (see Village Edinburgh, page 76). A pint of Lorimer and Clark's 80/- here is a must. They also serve good bar food and the restaurant is recommended. The athletic young ladies, if they are not currently banned, are from the nearby college of physical education. Good views over the estuary, and bracing walks along the shore. Open 12.00–15.00, 19.00–23.00 Mon–Sat; 12.30–15.30 Sun.

Ensign Ewart   E2
521 Lawnmarket. 031–225 7440. Very handy for the Castle, Lady Stair's House and Gladstone's Land this is definitely one of the best pubs on the Royal Mile. The cosy, beamy bar is decorated with military prints and paintings, and the seating is comfy, with some intimate alcoves. Drybrough Eighty is sold, and food is available at lunchtime. Ensign Ewart was a sergeant in the Royal North British Dragoons who became a hero when he captured the standard of the French 45th Regiment at Waterloo. It is from this that the eagle badge worn by the Royal Scots Greys is derived. You can visit his grave on the north side of the Castle Esplanade. It is not surprising that such a first-rate pub, centrally situated can get very busy from time to time. Folk music Sun, Tue and Thur evenings from 20.00. Open 09.30–24.00 Mon–Sat; 12.30–14.30, 18.30–23.00 Sun.

Fiddler's Arms   E5
9–11 Grassmarket. 031–229 2665. A very fine traditional bar of great character. Tall founts at the wooden bar dispense McEwan's 80/- by air pressure, and lunchtime food is served. Folk music on Mon evenings. Open 11.00–23.00 Mon–Sat; 12.30–14.30, 18.30–23.00 Sun.

Forrest Hill Bar (Sandy Bell's)   F6
25 Forrest Rd, just south of Greyfriars Bobby. 031–225 1156. A traditional corner bar and noted folk music centre. The ale is McEwan's 80/- and Younger's No 3. Open 11.00–01.00 Mon–Sat. 12.30–14.30, 18.30–23.00 Sun.

Green Mantle   G6
133 Nicolson St. 031–667 3749. Large, lively corner bar with plenty of chairs and tables. The choice of beers includes Arrol's 70/-, Broughton Greenmantle and Lorimer & Clark's 70/- and 80/-. Food is available at lunchtime. Open 11.00–24.00 Mon–Wed; 11.00–01.00 Thur & Fri; 11.00–23.45 Sat; 12.30–14.30, 19.00–23.00 Sun.

Greyfriars Bobby   F5
34 Candlemaker Row. 031–225 8300. A wood panelled city pub, which is worth a visit if you've come to see the 'wee dug' outside. Arrol's 70/- is the main ale, and food is available lunchtime and evening. Candlemakers' Hall is next door. Open 11.00–24.30 Mon; 11.00–01.00 Tue–Thur; 11.00–02.00 Fri; 12.30–02.30 Sat; 18.30–11.00 Sun.

Guildford Arms   F2
West Register St. 031–556 1023. A beautifully ornate pub designed by R. M. Cameron in 1896, with stained wood, mirrors, and a lofty ribbed ceiling which gives enough space for a theatrical gallery bar (but beware, it is sometimes closed). A cosy place decorated with antique maps and where you can view the

comings and goings downstairs. On the way up, look out for the amazing tiger mirror. Lorimer's 80/–, McEwan's 80/–, Younger's No 3 and Arrol's 70/– to choose from. Food is available at lunchtime Open 11.00–23.00 Mon–Sat; 12.30–14.30, 18.30–22.30 Sun.

Jolly Judge E4
James Court, off Lawnmarket. 031–225 2669. Much of the spirit of an early tenement building has been preserved in this low ceilinged basement tavern by Lady Stair's House. Ind Coope Burton ale is served – very drinkable, but a pity there is not also a Scottish brew available. Lunchtime food. One of the better Royal Mile pubs. Open 11.00–23.00 Mon–Sat; 12.30–14.30, 18.30–23.00 Sun.

Kay & Company (Kay's Bar) C2
39 Jamaica St. 031–225 1858. A truly civilised retreat: the barman wears a white shirt, a red bow tie and a smile; quiet classical music plays, the serious daily papers are provided and a real smoky coal fire burns in the stone grate. Barrels line the walls, the bar is burnished wood and the ceiling is dark red. Choose from Belhaven, Lorimer & Clark, McEwan's and Younger's No 3. The building is probably the only original left in Jamaica Street and was once a wine shop, as some of the fittings reveal. Pies and rolls are served at lunchtime, there is a comfy room at the back, and it is open all day. An essential New Town visit. Open 11.00–23.00 Mon–Thur, 11.00–23.45 Fri & Sat. Closed Sun.

Kenilworth C3
Rose St. 031–225 8100. An attractive, high ceilinged bar dating from 1899 with an ornately carved wooden central island decorated with bank notes and supporting a large number of potted plants. Excellent Arrol's 70/– and Ind Coope Burton ale plus food at lunch-

time. Open 11.00–23.00 Mon–Sat; 12.30–14.30, 18.30–23.00 Sun.

Kilderkin
125 Constitution St, Leith. 031–554 3268. A very large pub with a spacious, comfortable lounge, in the busy centre of Leith. Maclay 70/– and 80/– is served, and food is usually available. Open 12.00–24.00 Mon–Sat; 12.00–14.30 Sun.

Leslie's Bar
45 Ratcliffe Terrace. 031–667 5957. Lorimer & Clark 70/– and 80/–. Beautifully decorated pub, with wood panelling, a moulded plasterwork ceiling, colourful leaded glass and a grand clock. Some comfy settles and the omnipresent TV can be avoided. Open 11.00–23.00 Mon–Thur, 11.00–24.00 Fri & Sat; 12.30–14.30, 18.30–23.00 Sun.

Liberton Inn
Kirk Brae/Kirkgate. 031–664 3102. The saloon bar here is noted for its 1930s black vitrolite decor and matching lighting – a gem of its kind. The beer, McEwan's 70/– and 80/–, is also excellent. Open 11.00–23.30 Mon–Fri; 11.00–23.45 Sat; 12.30–14.30, 18.30–22.30 Sun.

Malt Shovel F4
13 Cockburn St. 031–225 6843. A dimly lit and comfortable pub with some cosy alcoves, where you can enjoy a varied range of real ales, including some quite unusual examples like Jennings Mild, from Cockermouth. There is also a vast array of single malt whiskies, and lunchtime food. Open 12.00–24.00 Mon–Thur; 12.00–01.00 Fri; 12.00–23.30 Sat; 12.30–14.30, 18.30–23.00 Sun.

H.P. Mather's Bar B4
Queensferry St. 031–225 3549. Original one room city bar, where the McEwan's 80/– is served by air pressure from tall founts. They also serve pies to the

mainly male clientele. *Open 11.00–24.00 Mon–Sat; 11.00–14.00, 19.00–23.30 Sun.*

Old Chain Pier

Trinity Crescent, Newhaven. 031–552 1233. Right on the sea front – indeed it is built on the site of the Old Chain Pier, which is beautifully illustrated on the sign outside. Windows behind the bar silhouette the staff against a wide vista of the Forth, with the low hills of Fife in the distance, making this a magical place at dusk on a fine evening. There is a little gallery decorated with old photographs and engravings. Drybrough Eighty is served, and there is food available at lunchtime. *Open 11.30–23.00 Mon–Thur, 11.30–24.00 Fri & Sat; 12.30–14.30, 18.30–23.00 Sun.*

Olde Inn

Main St (corner of Cramond Road South), Davidsons Mains. 031–336 2437. An excellent example of an Edinburgh suburban local, and very handy for Safeway. Belhaven 70/– and Drybrough Eighty are sold, as is lunchtime food. *Open 11.00–23.00 Mon–Sat; 12.30–14.30, 18.30–22.30 Sun. Oct–Mar closed 14.30–17.00 Mon–Thur.*

Peacock

Lindsay Rd, Newhaven. 031–552 8707. No longer a simple 17thC fisherman's retreat, this is now a nicely developed pub restaurant, with comfy bars, an attractive garden, and a reputation for outstanding fish and chips. There is other good food, of course, and a carvery, all approved by Les Routiers. McEwan's 80/–, is served by air pressure, as it should be in these parts. Family room. *Open 11.00–14.30, 17.00–23.00 Mon–Sat; 12.30–14.30, 18.30–23.00 Sun.*

Piershill Tavern (Porter's)

7 Piershill Place, Portobello Rd. 031–661 6661. There once was a time here when, if you were female, or English, or both, you would have felt distinctly uncomfortable amongst the hard drinking locals. Indeed this was once a 'men only' bar. Re-built after fire damage, it is now a worthwhile stop on the way to Portobello. Belhaven 80/– and Tennant Heriot 80/– served by air pressure, and food at lunchtime. *Open 11.00–23.00 Mon–Sat; 12.30–14.30, 18.30–23.00 Sun.*

Preservation Hall   E4

9 Victoria St, the top end. 031–226 3816. A fine conversion of a church hall, with an attractive bar and gantry. Plenty of space in which to enjoy your McEwan's 80/– or Younger's No 3 and a lunchtime meal. *Open 11.30–24.00 Mon–Wed; 11.30–01.00 Thur–Sat; 19.00–23.00 Sun.*

Raffles   C1

48/50 St Stephen St, Stockbridge. 031–225 5395. A popular basement bar under an antique shop, serving Belhaven 80/– all day (closed Sun). Just down the road is St Stephen's Church, a bizarre building by Playfair – best seen sober, since the effect if drunk is unnerving. Lunches are available. *Open 12.00–23.00 Mon–Sat. Closed Sun.*

Ryrie's Bar

Haymarket Station. 031–337 7582. Established in 1862, 18 years before the station which it complements so well – indeed you could miss a few trains if you became settled here. Beautifully traditional, with a fine gantry and stained glass windows. The beer is, of course, McEwan's 80/– and Younger's No 3. *Open 11.00–23.00 Mon–Wed; 11.00–24.00 Thur & Fri; 11.00–23.00 Sat; 12.30–14.30, 19.00–23.00 Sun.*

Scott's Bar   C3

202 Rose St. 031–225 7401. A low ceilinged Georgian lounge at the west end of Rose Street, handy for the shops and Charlotte Square. Belhaven 80/– and

Drybrough Eighty are available plus food is served at lunchtime. *Open 11.00–23.00 Mon–Wed; 11.00–24.00 Thur; 11.00–01.00 Fri; 11.00–24.00 Sat. Closed Sun.*

Sheep's Heid
Causeway, Duddingston Village. 031–661 1020. There are plenty of good reasons to visit this place – the walk from the city centre through Holyrood Park; the prettiness of the surrounding village and the wildfowl on the loch all make for an enjoyable outing, not withstanding the pleasures of the pub itself, an 18thC coaching inn whose licence dates from the 15thC. Inside it is panelled, carpeted and cosy, with dividing screens and an elegant bar. At the back, there is a garden and a skittle alley, a unique feature in these parts. Barbecues are held outside in fine weather. Indoors food includes filled rolls, soup and haggis. The beer to ask for is 'Sheep's Heid'; lunches are served. *Open 11.00–23.00 Mon–Sat; 12.30–14.30, 18.30–22.00 Sun.*

Shore
The Shore, Leith. 031–553 5080. A very attractive wine bar which is not that far removed from being a pub. Definitions are of little consequence, when the decor is as attractive as this: bentwood chairs, fine mirrors, bric-a-brac and palm trees, all in a beautiful situation by the harbour. McEwan's 80/–, excellent food and wine. Not so long ago respectable people avoided these parts . . . *Open 11.00–01.00 Mon–Sat. Closed Sun.*

Starbank Inn
64 Laverockbank Rd, Newhaven. 031–552 4141. A very handsome stone built pub with panoramic views over the Forth and decorated as a virtual museum of brewing. In keeping with this theme there is always a good choice of beer – Belhaven, Maclay and others – and all in

excellent condition. Bar meals are served and there is a good restaurant. *Open 11.00–23.00 Mon–Wed; 11.00–23.30 Thur–Sat; 12.30–14.30, 18.30–23.00 Sun.*

Tilted Wig
1 Cumberland St, Dundonald St end. 031–556 9409. Considered a rather up-market bar, it is included here because of its attractive beer garden, below the street at basement level, and quite unusual in the city. The beer here, Maclay 70/– and 80/– and Theakston's Best Bitter on handpump. The Bloody Marys are renowned here. Food is served in the back bar; typical starters are home-made pâté and soup followed by steak and kidney pie or casserole. *Open 11.00–14.30, 17.00–23.00 Mon–Thur; 11.00–01.00 Fri; 11.00–23.00 Sat. Closed Sun.*

Volunteer Arms (Canny Mans)
237 Morningside Rd. 031–447 1484. Belhaven 70/– and 80/– to enjoy among a fascinating collection of relics, adverts and bric-a-brac. Look out for the set of copper whisky jugs and measures, and the accounts book dated 1892–3. Lunches are served. Part of the old village of Morningside remains to be explored, and listen out for the 'refained' pronunciation heard around this respectable suburb. *Open 12.00–24.00 Mon–Sat; 12.30–14.30, 18.30–23.00 Sun.*

Ye Olde Golf Tavern
Wright's Buildings, off Bruntsfield Place, south of Tollcross. 031–229 5040. A very handsome and unusual pub dating from 1456, in an excellent situation overlooking Bruntsfield Links. Very well kept Belhaven 60/– and 80/– ale is served by air pressure from the unusual Reid 'tea urn' founts, and food is available until 19.00. The lounge is spacious and comfy. Well worth a brisk walk from George IV Bridge across The Meadows. *Open 11.30–24.00 Mon–Thur, 11.30–01.00 Fri & Sat; 12.30–14.30, 18.30–23.00 Sun.*

Drinking Out of Town

Aberlady, The Waggon
Main St, Aberlady, Lothian. (On the A198 towards Edinburgh). 087–57 204. A pleasant airy bar with fine views over Aberlady Bay towards Fife. Good bar food and restaurant meals L&D, Mc-Ewans 80/– real ale and family room. *Open 11.00–14.30, 18.00–23.00 Mon–Fri; 11.00–14.30, 17.00–23.00 Sat; 12.30–14.30, 18.30–23.00 Sun.*

Anstruther, Sun Tavern
Harbour Head, Anstruther, Fife. 033–331 0068. A salty old pub opposite the harbour and next door to the Scottish Fisheries Museum. McEwans real ale and some local seafood dishes. *Open 11.00–24.00 Mon–Sat; 12.30–14.30, 18.30–23.00 Sun.*

Dirleton, Castle Inn
Dirleton, Lothian. 062–085 221. Hospitable local with real fires and a fine collection of brewery mirrors. McEwans 80/– is served from tall founts, and bar food available all day. *Open 11.00–14.30, 17.00–23.00 Mon–Sat; 12.00–14.30, 18.30–23.00 Sun.*

East Linton, Linton Arms
5 Bridge St, East Linton, Lothian. 062–086 0298. A fine village pub conveniently close to Preston Mill, serving Ind Coope Burton real ale. *Open 11.00–23.00 Mon–Thur; 11.00–01.00 Fri; 11.00–24.00 Sat; 12.30–23.00 Sun.*

Elie, The Ship Inn
The Toft, Elie, Fife. 033–333 0246. A welcoming and comfortable wood panelled old pub over-looking the wide sweep of Elie harbour. Nautical decor and nautical clientele of dinghy sailors, yachtsmen and sail-boarders. Well situated garden, children allowed into back room. Open fires in winter and Belhaven real ale to sup. Bar snacks at lunchtime. *Open 11.00–24.00 Mon–Sat; 12.30–14.30, 18.30–23.00 Sun.*

Gifford, Tweeddale Arms
High St, Gifford, East Lothian. 062–081 240. Well situated facing the green in this very pretty village. A comfortable inn, with plenty of settees and chintzy chairs, an ideal place to enjoy McEwans 80/– real ale and excellent bar meals available all day. There is also an elegant dining room for full meals. Children welcome. *Open 11.30–23.00 Mon–Sat; 12.00–14.30, 18.30–23.00 Sun.*

Musselburgh, Volunteer Arms
79–81 North High St, Musselburgh, Lothian. A traditional wood panelled pub with a fine gantry, dispensing Mc-Ewans 80/– and Youngers real ale. *Open 11.00–14.30, 18.30–23.00 Mon–Sat; 12.30–14.30, 18.30–23.00 Sun.*

Newtongrange, Dean Tavern
80 Main St, Newtongrange, Lothian. 031–663 2419. A rare example of a reformed pub, built at the turn of the century and known as Goths, after a system which originated in Gothenburg, where all the profits passed to a local trust for the benefit of the local community. This one is well situated for the Scottish Mining Museum. Vast, cavernous, almost ecclesiastical, it serves Tennant 80/– real ale. This is the establishment mentioned in the Mining Museum's audio-tableaux display. *Open 11.00–14.30, 18.30–23.00 Mon–Sat; 12.30–14.30, 18.30–23.00 Sun.*

Pathhead, Forester's Arms
Main St, Pathhead, Lothian. 087–532 0273. A well modernised village local with an agricultural theme. McEwans 80/– and Youngers real ale is served, as well as good bar food. *Open 11.00–15.00,*

17.00–23.00 Mon–Sat; 12.30–15.00, 18.30–23.00 Sun.

Ratho, The Bridge Inn
27 Beird Rd, Ratho, Lothian. 031–333 1320. A canal-side pub decorated with prints depicting life on the Union Canal, which once linked Edinburgh with Glasgow. A restaurant boat leaves each evening, but the food in the land-based restaurant is just as good. Bar meals available all day and Belhaven real ale. Open 11.00–23.00 Mon–Sat; 12.30–14.30, 18.30–23.00 Sun.

St Andrews, The Grange Inn
Grange Rd, St Andrews, Fife. 033–472 670. Noted for its excellent and reasonably priced food, this fine old pub has an inglenook in the bar, and serves real ale. Open 12.00–14.30, 18.30–23.00 Tue–Sun; 18.30–23.00 Mon.

Stirling, Wallace
Airthrey Rd, Causewayhead, Stirling. 078–673 005. The downstairs bar is lively and full of character, upstairs it's quieter with views of the castle. Belhaven real ale. Open 11.00–23.00 Mon–Sat; 12.30–14.30, 18.30–23.00 Sun.

Wester Howgate, Old Howgate Inn
Wester Howgate, Lothian. 096–874 244. Cosy 18thC coaching inn with low ceilings and a log fire. The choice of real ales runs to four: Belhaven, Greenmantle, McEwans 80/– and Theakstons Best, and the adjacent restaurant is recommended. Open 11.00–14.30, 17.00–23.00 Mon–Sat; 12.00–14.30, 18.30–23.00 Sun.

Restaurants

There is no shortage of restaurants in Edinburgh offering an inventive choice of food. As well as traditional Scottish fare, you'll find a wide range of eateries from the cheap and cheerful (but tasty) Chinese and Indian to the noisy Italian and sophisticated French restaurant. You are certain to find somewhere you'll like at a price you can afford. No one could be disappointed eating out in Edinburgh.

Don't be surprised if the restaurant is a little way from the city centre – there are good places to eat all over town. Leith, also, offers a range of restaurants and wine bars in an historic waterfront setting.

Scotland is endowed with an abundance of natural produce, including partridge, grouse, pheasant, venison, salmon, trout, Aberdeen Angus beef, shellfish and herring – only a poor chef could fail to come up with a feast. A traditional Scottish dish is not necessarily haggis and neeps. An elaborate dinner could include smoked salmon, venison stew, roast beef or perhaps lobster from the Firth of Forth.

In the following selection of restaurants credit cards accepted are indicated as follows: A = Access, Ax = American Express, D = Diners Club, V = Visa (Barclaycard etc).

Price for a three-course meal for one without wine, but including VAT and service, is indicated thus: **£** – up to £8.00; **££** – from £8.00–15.00; **£££** – £15.00 and over. NB. Many restaurants are cheaper at lunchtime.

Cafés

Bagguley's
2 Deanhaugh St. 031–332 1469. A good range of homemade lunches, plus cakes, pastries and waffles in farmhouse kitchen surroundings. Wine, beer and hot toddys on offer. *Open 10.00–16.00 Mon–Sat. Closed Sun.* No credit cards. **£.**

Breadwinner
1 Raeburn Place, Stockbridge. 031–332 3864. Serves light lunches of pizza and quiche; delicious teas with wholemeal bread, pastries and gâteaux. Cheerful service and a choice of wines. *Open 09.30–17.00 Mon–Sat; 12.00–17.00 Sun.* No credit cards. **£.**

Clarinda's J3
69 Canongate. 031–557 1888. After walking the Royal Mile, this is a nice place to enjoy home-baking or a light lunch. Licensed. *Open 08.30–16.45 (18.00 summer) Mon–Sat; 10.00–16.45 Sun.* No credit cards. **£.**

Fruitmarket Gallery F3
29 Market St. 031–225 2383. Compact wholefood café above an art gallery. Good selection of vegetarian salads. The coffee is superb. *Open 10.00–17.00 Mon–Sat; 13.30–17.00 Sun. A.V.* **£.**

Gallery of Modern Art Café
Belford Rd. 031–556 8921. Well thought out, inventive, mainly vegetarian menu hidden in this bright basement café. Home baking. There is also a well chosen wine list. Outside terrace is delightful in warm weather. *Open 10.30–16.30 Mon–Sat; 14.00–16.30 Sun.* No credit cards. **£.**

Laigh Kitchen D2
117a Hanover St. 031–225 1552. Homely, unspoilt old kitchen, warmed by a real fire in winter. Serves good lunchtime salads, cakes and pastries. Worth looking out, although you'll often have to share a table when it's busy. *Open 08.30–16.00 Mon–Sat. Closed Sun and public hols.* No credit cards. **£.**

Lower Aisle F4
St Giles Cathedral, High St. 031–225 5147. Light lunches, all home baking. Not surprisingly unlicensed as it's in the crypt. *Open 10.00–16.30 Mon–Fri; 10.00–14.00 Sun. Closed Sat.* No credit cards. **£.**

Queen's Hall Café H7
South Clerk St. 031–668 3456. Mix with the musicians in this cheerful café serving well-prepared fresh salads, vegetarian dishes, puddings and cheese. Accompanied by a solid choice of wines. *Open 10.00–17.00 Mon–Sat (later on concert nights). Closed Sun.* No credit cards. **£.**

Round Table G3
31 Jeffrey St. 031–557 3032. Wholesome fare served in good quantities in earthenware vessels. Daily specials on the blackboard, hot dishes and salads as well as home-made soup home-baked cakes. Note the beautifully carved round wooden table, from which this café takes its name. *Open 10.00–17.30 Mon–Sat. Closed Sun.* No credit cards. **£.**

Chinese

Kweilin
19–21 Dundas St. 031–557 1875. Upmarket Cantonese eatery with an excellent range of seafood specialities and beef dishes, served by friendly and helpful staff. A worthwhile choice of wine, excellent value at lunchtime but prices definitely go up for the evening sitting. *Open 12.00–23.30 Mon–Thur; 12.00–24.30 Fri & Sat; 17.00–23.30 Sun. V.* **££.**

Loon Fung

2 Warriston Place, Broughton. 031–556 1781. Food is tastier than the decor. A large menu but speciality of the day recommended. Set menu less adventurous but reasonably priced. Limited wine list. Open 12.00–24.00 Mon–Thur; 12.00–01.00 Fri & Sat; 14.00–24.00 Sun. A.Ax.V. £.

Lune Town   A4

38 William St. 031–220 1688. Well known and thus often crowded Cantonese restaurant. Dim sum popular at lunchtime. Book to avoid being banished to the claustrophobic basement. Open 12.00–14.30, 18.00–24.00 Mon–Thur; 12.00–14.30, 18.00–01.00 Fri & Sat; 17.00–23.30 Sun. A.Ax.D.V. ££.

New Dragon Pearl   G1

20 Union Place. 031–556 4547. Some claim this is the best Cantonese cooking north of the border. The menu is exhaustive with a wide variety of seafood. Open 12.00–01.00 Mon–Sat; 12.00–23.00 Sun. No credit cards. ££.

New Edinburgh Rendezvous   B4

10a Queensferry St. 031–225 2023. Large traditional Pekinese restaurant, serving individual dishes as well as 10-course banquets. Large and reasonably priced wine list. Open 12.00–14.00, 17.30–23.30 Mon–Sat; 13.00–23.30 Sun. A.Ax.D.V. ££.

Yee Kiang

42 Dalmeny St. 031–554 5833. Friendly Pekingese restaurant in the front parlour of a Victorian tenement. Mouth-watering menu but a disappointing wine list. Open 17.00–01.00 Tue–Sun. Closed Mon. A.V. ££.

Country House Restaurants

Carlton Highland   F4

Carlton Hotel, North Bridge. 031–556 7277. Two grand restaurants here. Carlton Court is a self-service carvery and Quills has a menu built around fresh Scottish produce such as Aberdeen Angus beef. Some good wines. Open Carlton Court 12.00–14.30, 18.30–22.00 Mon–Sun; Quills 12.30–14.00, 19.00–22.00 Mon–Sun. A.Ax.D.V. ££.

George Hotel   E2

George St. 031–225 1251. Carvery is excellent with large helpings and ample vegetables. Good cheese board. Le Chambertin is an opulent, elegant French restaurant. Comprehensive wine list and first-class service. Open Carvery 12.30–14.00, 18.30–22.00 Mon–Sun; Le Chambertin 12.30–14.00, 19.00–22.00 Mon–Sun. A.Ax.D.V. ££.

Donmaree Hotel

21 Mayfield Gardens. 031–667 3641. No new-fangled cooking here. Traditional fare, such as roast beef, with a substantial and expensive wine list. Reasonably priced set menu at lunchtime. Open 12.30–14.00, 18.30–22.00 Mon–Fri; 18.30–22.00 Sat. Closed Sun. A.Ax.D.V. £££.

Gazebo   B4

Caledonian Hotel, Princes St. 031–225 2433. Excellent value 'help yourself' breakfasts – including kidneys and kippers. The lunchtime cold buffet is more expensive. Extensive international menu in the evening. Open 07.00–10.00, 12.00–14.30, 19.00–22.00 Mon–Sun. A.Ax.D.V. ££.

Howard Hotel   D1

32–36 Great King St. 031–557 3500. Warm and comfortable atmosphere in the restaurant, where the cuisine is based on fresh Scottish produce, including poached fillet of salmon in white wine. Good value set lunches and dinners. The delicious ice-cream comes from Lucas, the renowned Italian ice-cream makers at Musselburgh. For a light lunch go to the busy Claret Jug next door. *Open 12.00–14.00, 18.30–21.30 Mon–Fri; 18.30–21.00 Sat & Sun.* A.Ax. D.V. **££**.

Pompadour   B4

Caledonian Hotel, Princes St. 031–225 2433. Excellent large restaurant offering Scottish fare – smoked fish, mussel and onion brose – at lunchtime and the best of nouvelle cuisine during the evening. Classic wines. Expensive but not as steep at lunchtime. *Open 12.00–14.00, 19.00–22.30 Mon–Fri; 19.00–22.30 Sat & Sun.* A.Ax.D.V. **£££**.

Prestonfield House

Prestonfield Rd. 031–668 3346. An elegant and charming 17thC mansion, the past guest list reads like a who's who of history – Bonnie Prince Charlie, Benjamin Franklin and Dr Johnson have all been here. Set in acres of beautiful parkland inhabited by peacocks and Highland cattle. Imaginatively and carefully cooked international dishes. A la carte menu and specialities, which reflect the pick of the market – roast pheasant and wild duck for example. Naturally there is a more than adequate wine list. *Open 12.30–14.00, 19.00–21.30 Mon–Sun.* A.Ax.D.V. **£££**.

French

L'Auberge   G4

56 St Mary's St. 031–556 5888. Innovative French nouvelle cuisine in a stylish, luxurious, mirrored restaurant. Chef seems to excel at fish dishes. Wide choice of desserts, expensive wine list. Good and reasonably priced set lunch. *Open 12.15–14.00, 18.45–21.30 Mon–Fri; 12.15–14.00, 18.45–22.30 Sat. Closed Sun.* A.Ax.D.V. **£££**.

La Bagatelle   G5

221a Nicolson St. 031–667 0747. Base-

ment bistro with unpretentious and reasonably priced French fare, including seafood pancakes, in simple surroundings. Good but short wine list. *Open 12.00–14.00, 18.30–22.30 Mon–Sat; 12.30–15.30 Sun.* A.V. **£**.

Café de Paris, Hotel de France   F3

8–10 South St Andrew St. 031–556 8774. A slightly scruffy brasserie which offers a good range of simple snacks and meals as well as some more elaborate dishes – marinated prime beef fillet. Wine and French beer. Keeps real brasserie hours. *Open 08.00–04.00 Mon–Sun.* A.Ax.D.V. **£**.

Chez Julie

110 Raeburn Place, Stockbridge. 031–332 2827. Unassuming, friendly bistro serving simple but freshly prepared dishes including steaks and scampi. Popular with locals. *Open 12.00–14.00, 18.30–22.00 Mon–Sat; 18.30–22.00 Sun.* A.Ax.D.V. **££**.

Le Bouzy   C7

22a Brougham Place. 031–229 0869. Neat and tidy French restaurant, serving cuisine bourgeoise and nouvelle cuisine. Good choice of French wines. *Open 12.00–14.00, 18.30–22.30 Mon–Sat; 18.30–21.30 Sun.* A.Ax.D.V. **££**.

Le March Noir

2–4 Eyre Place. 031–558 1608. Bustling bistro atmosphere in a farmhouse setting. Adventurous Provençal menu which changes daily. Interesting wine list. *Open 12.00–14.00, 19.00–22.00 Mon–Sat. Closed Sun.* A.V. **££**.

Maxie's Bistro   G6

32 West Nicolson St. 031–667 0845. Lively bistro frequented by students; a small but varied menu including stuffed trout and pork in orange sauce, and a good range of inexpensive wines. Can be crowded at lunchtime. *Open 12.00–15.00,*

17.00–24.00 Mon–Sat; 17.00–23.00 Sun. A.V. **££**.

Merchants F5
17 Merchant St (known as Candlemaker Row). 031–225 4009. Smart airy restaurant beneath George IV Bridge, with classical but varied cuisine. Menu changes weekly. *Open* 12.30–14.30, 18.30–22.30 *Mon–Sat. Closed Sun.* A.Ax.D.V. **££**.

Le Sept F4
7 Old Fishmarket Close (off High St). 031–225 5428. Relaxed French restaurant and brasserie where you can enjoy a simple inexpensive lunch, such as crêpes and omelettes. A pleasant little oasis from the bustle of the Royal Mile. The more elaborate dinner menu is based on classic French cuisine with a speciality plat du jour. Book for seating on the small balcony. *Open* 12.00–14.30, 18.30–22.30 *Mon–Sat;* 18.30–22.30 *Sun.* A.D.V. **££** restaurant, **£** brasserie.

La Vinotheque
2–6 Bonnington Road Lane. 031–554 9113. Uncompromisingly French, with plenty of oil and garlic. The wines are specially imported by the proprietor. *Open* 12.00–14.00, 18.00–22.00 *Mon–Sat. Closed Sun.* No credit cards. **££**.

Grills
Champany Grill
2 Bridge Rd, Colinton. 031–441 2587. Some of Scotland's finest meat, expertly grilled, provides the basis of the menu, backed up with an array of salads, good veg and sauces. Black Forest Ham well smoked and served with hot butter and onion sauce makes an original starter. Standards are high so don't expect to get away with a small bill. *Open* 12.30–14.00, 19.00–21.45 *Mon–Sat. Closed Sun.* A.Ax.D.V. **£££**.

Indian

Ghandhi Tandoori G1
22 Union Place. 031–556 1521. Lively, above average Indian opposite the Playhouse. Serves standard dishes but all expertly prepared. *Open* 12.00–14.00, 17.00–24.00 Mon–Sun. A.Ax.D.V. **££**.

Kalpna G7
2–3 Patrick Sq. 031–667 9890. Excellent Gujerati and southern Indian vegetarian food, with a variety of traditional and innovative dishes. Lassi or Kingfisher beer. *Open* 12.00–14.00, 17.30–23.00 *Mon–Sat. Closed Sun.* A.V. **£**.

Lancers
5 Hamilton Place, Stockbridge. 031–332 3444. Deemed one of the top 30 curry houses in Britain. Bengali menu with special emphasis on vegetarian dishes. *Open* 12.30–14.30, 17.30–23.00 Mon–Sun. A.Ax.V. **£**.

Miahs
17–19 Forrest Rd. 031–225 7396. Good tikkas, tandooris and bhajias in this well decorated eatery near Greyfriars Bobby. Specialises in Kashmiri and Muglai cookery. *Open* 12.00–15.00, 17.30–24.00 Mon–Thur & Sun; 12.00–15.00, 17.30–01.00 Fri & Sat. A.Ax.V. **£**.

The Raj
Henderson St, Leith. 031–553 3980. Restrained, above-average decor in this suave restaurant, where some fine Bengali cuisine is served. Good wine list. *Open* 12.00–14.30, 17.30–23.30 Mon–Sun. A.Ax.V. **££**.

Shamiana D7
14 Brougham St. 031–228 2265. Short, inventive menu in this unusual but outstanding North Indian restaurant. One of the best Indians around and conven-

ient for the King's Theatre. *Open 12.00–14.00, 18.00–23.30 Mon–Sat. Closed Sun.* A.Ax.D.V. **£££**.

Verandah Tandoori
17 Dalry Rd. 031–337 5828. Up-market North Indian and Bangladeshi cooking, with one or two outstanding dishes. Wine list not as good as the food but there's always beer. *Open 12.00–14.30, 17.00–23.45 Mon–Sun.* A.Ax.D.V. **££**.

International

Brasserie Saint Jacques　　　　　F2
King James Thistle Hotel, Leith St. 031–556 0111. A straightforward menu built around Scottish produce, such as oysters and Aberdeen Angus beef. Offers a generous selection of sweets such as hot rice pudding with Drambuie cream and bread and butter pudding. Also a French regional menu in this elegant and restrained hotel restaurant. Good value brasserie at lunchtime. *Open 12.30–14.00, 18.30–22.30 Mon–Sun.* A.Ax.D.V. **££–£££**.

Martins　　　　　C3
70 Rose St, North Lane. 031–225 3106. Attractive restaurant hidden among the warehouses off Rose Street, but it's worth the search. Only uses fresh and top-quality ingredients such as venison, cooked to order. Not cheap. *Open 12.00–14.00, 19.00–22.00 Tue–Sat. Closed Sun & Mon.* A.Ax.D.V. **££**.

Vintner's Room
The Vaults, 87 Giles St, Leith. 031–554 6767. Well-presented dishes including wild poached salmon with watercress soufflé all served in a room used since the early 1600s to sell claret which came into Leith from France. Naturally the wine list is excellent. *Open 12.00–14.00, 18.30–23.30 Mon–Sat. Closed Sun.* A.Ax.D.V. **£££**.

Italian

Bar Napoli　　　　　E3
75 Hanover St. 031–225 2600. Friendly basement pizza house. Open for late-night scoff. *Open 12.00–02.00 Sun–Thur; 12.00–03.00 Fri & Sat.* A.Ax.D.V. **£**.

Bar Roma　　　　　B4
39a Queensferry St. 031–226 2977. Basic, earthy Italian with friendly atmosphere, where the pasta and pizza are the best value. Popular with those who enjoy the impromptu staff entertainment. *Open 12.00–02.00 Mon–Sun.* A.V. **£**.

Caprice
327 Leith Walk. 031–554 1279. Good value restaurant with a well founded reputation for serving the best pizzas in town. *Open 12.00–14.00, 17.30–23.00 Mon–Thur; 12.00–14.00, 17.30–23.30 Fri & Sat; 18.00–23.00 Sun.* A.Ax.D.V. **£**.

Cosmo's　　　　　C3
58a North Castle St. 031–226 6743. Long-established trattoria with simple, proficient and delicious Italian fare. Reasonable wine list. *Open 12.30–14.30 Tue–Fri; 18.30–22.00 Sat. Closed Sun & Mon.* A.V. **££**.

Duncan's Land　　　　　B1
8 Gloucester St, Stockbridge. 031–225 1037. Small attractive restaurant in 17thC house. The owner is also the chef, and his care is reflected in the fine Italian food he serves. Advisable to book. *Open 12.00–14.00, 18.30–22.00 Tue–Sat. Closed Sun & Mon.* A.V. **££**.

Raffaelli　　　　　B3
10 Randolph Place. 031–225 6060. Open all afternoon. The menu rarely changes but the wine list does, revealing proprietor's real interest. To really sample the wine go to the wine bar next door. *Open 12.00–21.30 Mon–Fri; 18.00–22.00 Sat. Closed Sun.* A.Ax.D.V. **££**.

Ravello
86 Morningside Rd. 031–447 9724. Simple, Italian cuisine with good fresh pasta and seafood dishes. It is possible to have a good, cheap meal which might explain its popularity. Some fine Italian wines. *Open 17.30–23.45 Tue–Sat. Closed Sun & Mon.* No credit cards. **££**.

Ristorante Milano   E4
7 Victoria St. 031–226 5260. A long, narrow restaurant decorated with old prints of Italy. Inventive Italian food: there's even swordfish on the menu. Unfortunately the sweet trolley is disappointing. *Open 12.00–14.00, 18.30–22.00 Mon–Sat; 18.30–22.00 Sun.* A.Ax.D.V. **££**.

Vito's   D3
55a Frederick St. 031–225 5052. Authentic, bustling Italian, with emphasis on seafood dishes. Crema di Gamberetti, cream of prawn soup, would make a good starter. Deserves its popularity as its food is to a high standard and not too expensive for its situation. Wine, mostly non-vintage, is served in pottery goblets. *Open 12.00–14.00, 18.00–23.00 Mon–Sat. Closed Sun.* A.Ax.D.V. **££**.

Mexican

Tex Mex   E3
38 Hanover St. 031–225 1796. Texan and Mexican dishes on offer. Choice of food is authentic and good and not all hot and spicy. *Open 12.00–01.00 Mon–Sat; 13.00–22.30 Sun.* A.V. **£**.

Viva Mexico   F3
Anchor Close, off Cockburn St. 031–226 5145. An atmospheric restaurant if your palate can take the hot, spicy dishes such as tacos, enchiladas and tortillas. Mexican music. *Open 12.00–14.30, 18.30–22.30 Mon–Sat. Closed Sun.* A.Ax.V. **£**.

Scottish

Howtowdie
25a Stafford St. 031–225 6291. Howtowdie is the old Scottish word for young chicken. Chicken howtowdie is included in a special Scottish menu. There is a wide range of entrees and fish dishes, also a venison lamlash. There is also a more expensive à la carte menu. *Open 12.00–14.00, 19.00–23.00 Mon–Fri; 19.00–23.00 Sat. Closed Sun.* A.Ax.D.V. **£££**.

Willis's   C3
Young Street Lane South. 031–225 3003. Or you can enter through 135a George Street. Good, straightforward filling fare for breakfast. Lunch menu on the blackboard – provides an extensive range of bar snacks and hot meals, including haggis and neeps. All baking done on the premises. Wide range of malt whiskies. *Open 08.00–17.00 Mon–Fri; 08.00–15.00 Sat. Closed Sun.* No credit cards. **£**.

Scottish Evenings

There are, for the benefit of visitors, several arranged 'Scottish Evenings'. Here one can enjoy a Scottish meal surrounded by a wealth of tartan, watch Highland dancing and listen to the pipes. Make sure to book in advance – they're popular.

George Hotel   E2
George St. 031–225 1251. Mon, *Wed*, Thur, Fri & Sun.

Gibby's Ceilidh
Learmonth Hotel, 18–20 Learmonth Terrace. 031–343 2671. Mon–Sun.

Jamie's Scottish Evening   F2
King James Thistle Hotel, Leith St. 031–556 0111. Sun–Fri.

Round Stables
Prestonfield House, Prestonfield Rd. 031–668 3346. Off Dalkeith Rd, beyond the Royal Commonwealth pool. Sun–Fri.

Dalhousie Courte
Cockpen, ·Bonnyrigg. 031–663 5155. Mon–Sun.

Ceilidhs
A ceilidh, with piping, song and dance can be arranged for private groups. Ring 031–661 6038 for details.

Seafood

Café Royal Oyster Bar   F2
17 West Register St. 031–556 4124. Plenty of Victorian stained glass and wood in this classic seafood restaurant. Fresh produce all carefully cooked in rich, tasty sauces. The house wine is François Aliane's reliable Alliance. *Open* 12.00–14.00, 19.00–22.30 Mon–Sun. A.V. **£££**.

Cousteau's   D2
109 Hanover St. 031–226 3355. Pleasant, modern fish restaurant with, unfortunately only a limited range of vegetables and sweets on the menu. *Open* 18.30–23.00 Mon–Sat. *Closed Sun.* A.Ax.D.V. **££**.

Cramond Inn
Glebe Rd, Cramond. 031–336 2035. Whitewashed building in an attractive village setting where the River Almond enters the Firth of Forth. Specialising in conventional seafood, such as whitebait. Bar food. *Open* 12.30–14.00, 18.30–22.00 Mon–Sat; 12.30–14.00 Sun. A.Ax.D.V. **££**.

Scots
8–10 Eyre Place. 031–556 1177. Fish is the main, but not the exclusive theme of the restaurant. Set lunch is particularly good value. *Open* 17.00–22.00 Mon–Sat. *Closed Sun.* A.D.V. **££**.

Shrimps
107 St Leonard St. 031–667 9160. Cosy little Danish seafood restaurant, serving mostly open sandwiches in a Victorian front room, with an open fire on cold days. Wine list is good but limited. *Open* 11.00–15.00 Mon–Sat. *Closed Sun.* No credit cards. **£**.

Spanish

Parador
Queensway Hotel, 1 Queensferry Rd. 031–332 6492. An interesting and lively Spanish restaurant, with an outstanding range of seafood dishes. The Spanish wines are excellent. *Open* 12.30–14.30, 17.00–22.30 Mon–Sun. A.Ax.D.V. **££**.

Swiss

Alphorn
167 Rose St. 031–225 4787. Excellent German-Swiss cooking in slightly austere surroundings. Cow bells and a real alpine horn hang from the walls. Air-dried meats and sausages, classic Swiss starters, are very good here. Expensive but interesting wine list, including Swiss wines, with background information on each one. *Open* 12.00–14.00, 18.30–22.00 Tue–Sat. *Closed Sun & Mon.* A. **££**.

Wholefood & Vegetarian

Country Kitchen   C4
4–8 South Charlotte St. 031–220 1700. Licensed wholefood restaurant, with an excellent vegetarian choice. Ingredients and calories are listed on the menu (so you know how far you have to run to work it all off). Occasional piano player. *Open* 08.00–17.30 *(later in summer)* Mon–Sun. No credit cards. **£**.

Helios Fountain
7 Grassmarket. 031–229 7884. Genuinely wholesome vegetarian restaurant where all ingredients are fresh, natural and organic. No alcohol but excellent tea. Open 10.00–18.00 Mon–Sat. Closed Sun. A.Ax.V. **£**.

Henderson's   D2
94 Hanover St. 031–225 2131. Popular, basement self-service eatery with modern art decor and occasional live music. Plenty of choice, enough to fill any hungry vegetarian. Real ale, wine and separate wine bar. Get there early at lunchtime. Open 08.00–23.00 Mon–Sat. Closed Sun. V. **£**.

Wine Bars

Doric   F4
15 Market St. 031–225 5243. Simple bistro-cum-wine bar offering a range of fish dishes, with some good wines. Open 12.00–01.00 Mon–Wed; 12.00–02.00 Thur–Sat; 18.30–23.00 Sun. A.Ax.D.V. **££**.

Edinburgh Wine Bar   D2
110 Hanover St. 031–220 1208. Wonderful choice of wines, and a competent range of food. Friendly and relaxed atmosphere. Open 12.00–24.00 Mon–Wed; 12.00–01.00 Thur–Sat; 18.30–23.00 Sun. A.Ax.D.V. **£**.

Handsel's Wine Bar   A4
22 Stafford St. 031–225 5521. Elegant and cheerful wine bar downstairs, serving some excellent and imaginative food. The upstairs restaurant is more expensive. Open 11.30–23.00 Mon–Sat. Closed Sun. A.Ax.D.V. **£**.

Lilligs Weinstube   E4
30 Victoria St. 031–225 7635. Upstairs wine bar with a good range of European wines and Polish vodkas. Pub-type lunches. Open 11.00–23.00 Mon–Sun. Ax.V. **£**.

Shore Bar
3 The Shore, Leith. 031–553 5080. An excellent seafood restaurant-cum-wine bar by the Water of Leith. Wine good value. Often live music in the evenings. Open 11.00–24.00 Mon–Sat. Closed Sun. No credit cards. **££**.

Skipper's Bistro
1a Dock Place, Leith. 031–554 1018. Another of Leith's cheerful, but not so cheap, restaurant/wine bars. Accent on seafood. Much of the atmosphere of this old dockside pub remains. Open 12.30–14.00, 19.30–22.00 Mon–Sat. Closed Sun. A.Ax.V. **££**.

Waterfront Wine Bar
1c Dock Place, Leith. 031–554 7427. An interesting dockside bar, once an old waiting room where passengers sat before boarding the Aberdeen packet. Good reputation so tends to get very busy. Mainly barbecues in the summer, traditional home-baking in the winter. Extensive wine list and real ale. Open 11.00–23.00 Mon–Thur; 11.00–01.00 Fri–Sat. Closed Sun except for lunch in Jun, Jul & Aug. No credit cards. **£**.

Whigham's Wine Cellars
13 Hope St. 031–225 8674. Basement wine bar with authentic sawdust on the floor. Fresh casseroles, pickled fish and beef and oyster pie are among the delights on offer. Mature selection of wines. Open 11.00–12.00 Mon–Thur; 11.00–01.00 Fri & Sat. Closed Sun. V. **£**.

Eating Out of Town

Anstruther, Fife. The Cellar
24 East Green. 033–331 0378. Superb local seafood dishes are the basis of the menu, served in a cottagey sea-front res-

Restaurants

taurant. Set four-course dinner may include shellfish soup and halibut inventively sauced. Well chosen wine list. *Open 12.30–14.00, 19.00–21.30 Tue–Sat; 19.00–21.30 Mon. Closed Sun.* A.Ax.V. **£££**.

Cleish, Tayside. Nivingston House
057–752 16. Superbly prepared local produce and the judicious use of rich sauces combine beautifully in this hospitable country house hotel. Pheasant with black cherry and brandy is a favourite. Good bar meals at lunchtime. *Open 12.00–14.00, 19.00–21.00 Mon–Sun.* A.Ax.D.V. **£££**.

Cupar, Fife. Ostlers Close
25 Bonnygate. 033–455 574. Fresh local fish and game are the cornerstone of the menu, such as venison with blackcurrants. Excellent vegetables, all home grown. Long wine list. *Open 12.00–14.00, 18.00–21.30 Tue–Sun. Closed Mon.* A.V. **££**.

Dirleton, Lothian. Open Arms Hotel
062–085 241. Attractive coastal hotel with restaurant overlooking the village green. Good value lunches, with Scottish specialities such as mussel and onion stew or cranachan and blackcurrants. The food is more elaborate, and expensive during the evening. *Open 12.30–14.00, 19.30–22.00 Mon–Sun.* A.Ax.D.V. **££**.

Dunfermline, Fife. New Victoria
2 Bruce St. 038–372 4175. A big, old fashioned upstairs room overlooking the abbey, serving excellent and inexpensive traditional food, with delicious sweets and puddings. Teas and snacks throughout the day. *Open 09.30–18.00 Mon–Sat. Closed Sun.* No credit cards. **£**.

Falkland, Fife. Kind Kyttocks Kitchen.
Cross Wynd. 033–757 477. Everything fresh, wholesome and local – home cured ham, free range eggs, home-made bread. Basic wine list. *Open 10.30–17.30 Mon–Sun.* No credit cards. **£**.

Gullane, Lothian. La Potiniere
Main St. 062–084 3214. The name means gossip shop. Reputed for its freshly prepared soups, well balanced main courses accompanied by a superb wine list. Worth the drive. *Open 13.00–14.30 Mon–Fri & Sun; 13.00–14.30, 18.00–20.00 Sat.* No credit cards. **£££**.

Haddington, Lothian. Browns Hotel
1 West Rd. 062–082 2254. Restaurant in a beautiful Georgian house. Interesting but limited French menu and a short inexpensive wine list. *Open 18.00–21.00 Mon–Sun.* A.Ax.V. **££**.

Ingliston, Newbridge. Norton House Hotel
031–333 1275. Pleasant setting in extensive grounds and delightful ambience in the restaurant. The menu is ambitious and varied but generally successful. Friendly service. *Open 12.00–14.00, 18.00–21.30 Mon–Sun.* A.Ax.D.V. **££**.

Linlithgow, Lothian. Champany Inn
Champany Corner. 050–683 4532. Good quality steaks, chops and burgers, home-made sausages and pizzas. *Open 12.00–14.00, 18.00–22.00 Mon–Sat. Closed Sun.* A.Ax.D.V. **£**.

Peat Inn, Fife. Peat Inn
033–484 206. A highly rated restaurant where only fresh Scottish produce is lovingly prepared. Try the Tay salmon in vermouth sauce with chives. The wine list will not disappoint either. *Open 12.00–14.00, 18.00–21.30 Tue–Sat. Closed Sun.* Ax.D.V. **£££**.

Peebles, Borders.
Sunflower Coffee Shop
6 Bridgegate. 072–122 420. A tiny, homely, predominantly vegetarian restaurant tucked away behind the main street. Good stuffed pancakes and quiche. *Open 10.00–17.30 Mon–Sun.* No credit cards. **£**.

Restaurants

Wester Howgate, Lothian. Old Howgate Inn.
096–874 244. Danish restaurant in cosy 18thC inn with a log fire. Wide choice of open sandwiches available such as smoked chicken with asparagus · or mushroom and lemon mayonnaise. A Danish speciality is offered each evening.

Open 11.30–14.30, 18.00–22.00 Mon–Sat; 12.30–14.30, 18.30–22.00 Sun. A.Ax.D.V. £.

Uphall, Lothian. Houstoun House
050–685 3831. Salmon, pheasant, spring lamb give second place to a prodigious wine list. Menu changes. Open 12.00–14.00, 18.00–21.30 Mon–Sun. A.Ax.D. ££.

Nightclubs

The Amphitheatre B4
31 Lothian Rd. 031–229 7670. Edinburgh's premiere nightclub. Exclusive–360 degree lazers illuminate a split-level dance floor and a 20m long bar. Arrive before midnight to see the back wall open up to display the spectacular lazer/light show. *Open 22.00–04.00 Fri–Sun.*

Buster Browns F4
25–7 Market St. 031–226 4224. This is a small, intimate club quiet on Sundays but the bar definitely needs improving. *Open 22.30–04.00 Fri–Sun.*

Cinderellas Rockerfellas
99 St Stephen St. 031–556 0266. Situated in the cosy Stockbridge district, Cinders contains a restaurant and disco with 12 video screens backing up interesting music selections. *Open 23.00–03.00 Tue–Sun.*

Coasters C6
3 West Tollcross. 031–228 3252. This complex actually contains three clubs on each night, with everything from reggae to funk and eurobeat for the 20s upwards. *Open 23.30–04.00 Fri–Sun.*

Dillengers C4
28 King's Stables Rd. 031–228 3547. An innovative videotech with young

ideas situated in comfortably plush surroundings. *Open 22.00–04.00 Thur–Sun.*

Edgars C3
96a Rose St, North Lane. Interesting layout with passages and alcoves and probably the most expensive air-cooling system in the city. *Open 22.00–04.00 Thur–Sun.*

Fire Island Disco D3
127 Princes St. 031–226 4660. Well-established gay disco housing a clever lighting system. *Open 23.30–03.00 Mon–Sun.*

Madisons G1
The Playhouse, Greenside Place. 031–557 3807. A clever variety of music and an eye for an event easily outweigh Madison's dull shape and lay out. *Open 22.00–03.00 Thur–Sun.*

The Mission E4
Victoria St. 031–225 3326. Containing two venues, The Mission is lively, different and very popular at the weekend. *Open 22.30–03.00 Wed–Sun.*

Zenatec C6
56 Fountainbridge. 031–229 7733. Old hands at the disco game, Zenatec dazzles with lights and lazers in a comfortable well equipped club. *Open 22.30–03.00 Fri–Sun.*

Casinos

Casino Martell
7 Newington Rd. 031–667 7763. The atmosphere here is relaxed and informal. Try your hand at American Roulette and Blackjack. Restaurant and bar. *Open 22.00–04.00 Mon–Fri (02.00 Sat).*

Royal Chimes Casino Club   H1
3 Royal Terrace. 031–556 1055. Small intimate casino with restaurant and cocktail bar. American Roulette, Blackjack and Punto Banco. *Open 14.00–04.00 Mon–Fri; 14.30–04.00 Sat; 19.30–04.00 Sun.*

Stakis Regency Club   G1
14 Picardy Place. 031–557 3585. Plush, tastefully decorated casino with excellent restaurant and bar. Blackjack, Roulette and Punto Banco. *Open 12.00–04.00 Mon–Fri; 19.00–02.00 Sat; 21.00–04.00 Sun.*

The Berkley Casino
2 Rutland Place. 031–228 4446. New, up-market casino. Blackjack, American Roulette, Punto Banco plus Kalonki and Mah jong rooms. Membership. *Open 14.00–04.00 Mon–Sat; 19.30–04.00 Sun.*

Traditional Scottish Products

Scottish crafts and traditional merchandise, such as tartan, tweed, the pipes, whisky and haggis, can still be found all round Edinburgh today. What follows explains their history and true place in Scottish traditional life.

The Great Highland Bagpipe

The importance of the Great Highland Bagpipe to the Scottish psyche should not be underestimated. It demands great skill and much practice to play, and a suitable arena to float the sound. Its ancestry can be traced back to the simple reed pipe. A hollow reed or straw, flattened at one end and blown with pursed lips will emit a crude musical note. The bagpipes consist of three pipes, or drones (one bass, two tenor), a blow pipe with a mouthpiece, and a further pipe cut with finger holes upon which the notes can be varied. This is called the chanter. These are all attached to a bag of sheepskin or cowhide acting as a reservoir of air and enabling the typical unbroken sound to be produced. Of course, the pipes are no longer made of straw. Hardwoods are now used – laburnum, rosewood, African blackwood or Canadian maple – embellished with plastic, ivory or silver, depending on what you are prepared to pay. These components, properly cared for, will last for ever but the bag itself has to be replaced every two or three years, more often if it is not exercised by regular playing.

Although the Romans brought with them a form of bagpipe, it is thought that the Great Highland Bagpipe has developed from those brought by migrants from Ancient Egypt.

Each Highland Chieftan had as part of his entourage, an hereditary harpist (to play the Celtic harp) and an hereditary piper, who was given a ghillie to carry his pipes, and a house and land rent-free. At weddings and funerals, births and celebrations the pipes would be heard. Their rhythmic music would also encourage rowers crossing the Minch and later, as clan warfare became endemic, its stirring tones would carry above the tumult of battle.

Musical skills were passed from generation to generation with the establishment of piping families with some, such as that of the MacCrimmons of Skye, attaining a status owing more to legend than fact. A repertoire of serious music evolved, known as piobaireachd or ceol mor, meaning great music. Little music, ceol beag or ceol aotrom, as it is known today, was treated with disdain, although these airs, reels and strathspeys have once again found an appreciative audience.

Following the defeat of the Bonnie Prince at Culloden Field in 1745 the Disarming Act proscribed the use of the bagpipes (and tartan) classifying them as instruments of war. However, the Highland regiments, formed in 1757, were allowed the use of the pipes, and when the Disarming Act was repealed in 1782 the Great Highland Bagpipe reasserted its traditional role which continues to this day. The massed pipes played at the Edinburgh Royal Military Tattoo and the smaller local bands playing at Highland Games and ceremonials are an essential ingredient of Scotland's heritage. Drifting over the open hills, the skirl of the pipes is the ultimate evocation of all things Scottish.

Suppliers:

Clan Bagpipes E4
13a James Court, Lawnmarket (Royal Mile). 031–225 2415.
Discount Highland Supply E5
7 Cowgatehead, Grassmarket. 031–225 2390.
William Sinclair & Son
1 Madeira St. 031–554 3489.

Haggis

Recipe: take the heart, lungs and liver of a sheep, and boil for three hours with some beef fat. Allow to cool, skim off the fat, and mince. Take oatmeal, onion, gravy from the boiling, a liberal sprinkling of salt and pepper, and mix with the mince. Take one sheep's stomach (large haggis) or a length of large intestine (small haggis) and fill this with the mixture. Close it using cotton thread and blanket stitch. Return this to the boiler for a short while, when the membrane will shrink closely over its contents. Simmer for a further one and a half hours wrapped in foil before you serve. Split the haggis open lengthways and spoon out the contents piping hot, accompanied only by tatties (mashed potato) and champit neap (mashed turnip). Alternatively, go to any good Edinburgh butchers and buy one ready prepared, though often these days enclosed in plastic, which is fine for all except the purists, and preferable for the squeamish. The flavour is good and its nutritional value high.

Essential eating on Burns night (25 January), St Andrew's Day (30 November) and Hogmanay (31 December), deviations such as haggis burgers and Haggis and chips should be steadfastly avoided! Non-meat eaters will find an excellent vegetarian haggis available in Jenners Food Hall, Princes Street. The specialist supplier is:

Charles Macsween & Son
130 Bruntsfield Place. 031–229 1216.

Scotch Whisky

Ask any knowledgeable Scotsman for advice on choosing a single malt whisky, and his response will almost certainly be 'it is a very big subject'. For although whisky is available worldwide, it is the popular blends of grain and malt spirits that you will find acceptable when mixed with dry ginger or soda but without the depth of character, individuality or smoothness of a single malt. So what is the difference, and why all the fuss? 'Uisge-beagh', the Gaelic 'water of life', has been distilled in crofts in the Highlands and the Lowlands for many hundreds of years. Using only barley, peat and pure water, the process divides into two stages – brewing and distilling. Initially the barley is steeped in water and allowed to germinate. This is then gently dried over a smouldering peat fire, with the smoke permeating the malted barley and imparting a distinctive flavour. After grinding, it is mixed with water in a process known as mashing. The resultant sugary liquid, known as maltose, is then fermented with yeast, producing a crude alcohol known as wash, with a strength of about 12%. The second process, distilling, is carried out in a still, basically a copper vessel. The brew is heated in the still, with a coiled copper pipe or worm passing through cold water, in which the alcohol vapour will condense back into liquid – a very strong, colourless and crude whisky. After a further distillation it is mixed with water and allowed to mature in wooden casks (traditionally sherry casks to impart the characteristic golden colour) for a minimum of three years, usually at least eight years and often 10 years or more. During this time it mellows and matures, the flavour develops and it becomes smoother. The 'angels share' of one and a half percent is lost each year in evaporation. Once bottled whisky will not improve further, so is ready to drink right away.

This process, long and costly, results in products so individual that distilleries only yards apart, using the same ingredients, will produce completely different flavours. Single malt whisky should be drunk on its own, or diluted if you wish only with a little pure spring water. You will discover your own favourites by sampling various brands, but those to look out for are Laphroaig, a dark, aromatic peaty malt from Islay; Highland Park, a lighter peaty malt from Orkney, and Glenmorangie from Tain, a more widely available but justly popular product. When ordering, ask for them by name never just 'whisky' or 'Scotch'.

The popular blends, while still superbly consistent products, are made by a continuous, and therefore less costly, distillation process using a mixture of unmalted cereals such as maize, with some single malt whiskies mixed in to add flavour. Between 15 and 50 grain and malt whiskies may be used in a blend, and it is these products which account for 98% of Scotland's production. In the bleak, damp, windy Highland winters the richness of a malt whisky provided warmth and comfort in an inhospitable environment. It also helped to celebrate a marriage or a birth, and saw the dead on their way. It was even a medicine for the sick.

Sample as many single malts as is prudent, and choose a bottle or two to remind you of this inimitable aspect of Scottish tradition. The following suppliers offer a good choice, from a 43-year-old Linkwood at around £54 per bottle to the Original Oldbury Sheep Dip at around £13.

Lambert Brothers   D3
9–11 Frederick St (off Princes St). 031–225 4624.

William Cadenhead   J3
172 Canongate (Royal Mile). 031–556 5864.

Tartan, the Clans and Ancestral Research

You will see tartan carpets and curtains, tablecloths and napkins, book jackets and bagpipes, socks and hats, tee shirts and dolls, food wrappers and beer mats, scarves, jackets, and of course kilts. Over used and over done, you can't escape it, yet its traditional clan mystique is dubious, and its derivation is now throught to be from the French 'tiretaine', a woollen material, rather than from the Gaelic 'breacan'.

The weaving of cloth from sheep's wool is an ancient craft practised world-wide. Manufactured on a local basis in Scotland, it would have been coloured using natural plant dyes; consequently the material in one area would differ from that of another. The tartan became so strongly identified with the Highlanders that it was banned under the Disarming Act of 1747. Those 18thC tartans, surviving fragments reveal, bear hardly any resemblance to the material sold today.

A revival in interest of all things Scottish in the early 19thC brought with it the publication of a vast book, *The Costumes of the Clans* by the Sobieski Stuart brothers, who claimed to be the grandsons of the Bonnie Prince. By 1860 a whole new industry was established, and there are now some 500 clan tartans, one of which you are entitled to wear if you have the correct name, or the correct ancestors.

Its most handsome manifestation is in the kilt, which uses about 8m of material. Women wear a kilted skirt, made from 6m of cloth. With the correct complementary clothing it is a fine form of dress. You will see many shops selling tartan clothing and goods. One of the most highly regarded is:

Kinloch Anderson   G4

John Knox House, 45 High St (Royal Mile). 031–556 6961.

If you would like to find out if you are entitled to wear a Clan Tartan, and what that tartan should be, visit the:

Clan Tartan Centre

James Pringle Woollen Mill, 70–74 Bangor Rd, Leith. 031–553 5100.

To help research your Scottish ancestors, contact:

Scottish Roots   C3

1 Castle St. 031–226 2028.

Tweed

The finest tweed is Harris tweed, which can only be sold as such if it is made in the Outer Hebrides from virgin Scottish wool, woven on hand-looms in the weavers' own homes. It must also bear the orb trademark of the Harris Tweed Association, founded in 1909.

This hard-wearing, warm and water-resistant cloth was originally produced for the crofters' own use, until its wider applications were promoted by the wives of the wealthy landowners, such as Lady Dunmore of Amhuinnsuidhe Castle, Harris. Recent attempts to rationalise production by using larger power looms were strongly resisted by 95% of the weavers, who voted in the late 1970s to retain traditional methods and protect their quality of life and independence. But things have changed since the early days when the wool was sheared, dyed with crotal (natural dyes made from lichen) over a peat fire, carded and spun at the croft – all of this has been carried out at the factory in Stornoway since 1934. Indeed, the only person still producing tweed by traditional methods is Marion Campbell of Plocrapool, Harris, who still spins and dyes her own wool in the original way.

There are about 650 weavers on Lewis and Harris who produce some 4.5 million metres annually, using skills passed on from generation to generation. If you buy a garment made from this attractive and durable material, you will have a part of a great Scottish tradition that will repay its cost many times over.

Supplier:

Jenners   E3

Princes St. 031–225 2442. Sell lengths of Harris tweed in the lower ground floor, and tweed jackets on the upper ground floor.

Shopping in Edinburgh

Shopping in Edinburgh is a pleasure. Princes Street, the 'high street' of the city, has a variety of shops and department stores on the north side and on the south side the gardens, which give an uninterrupted view of the Castle. Of course, the major chain stores are now little different from their counterparts in any other town or city, but the jewel in the crown of Princes Street is Jenners, which is worth visiting at any time, both for the range of goods carried, and the architectural excellence of the building. Just across the road the Waverley Market is a new development of small, mainly specialist shops on different levels all under a translucent roof. With plenty of space to wander, and enlivened with some exotic plants, a fountain, small stalls, a wine bar, café and delicatessen, it is well worth a visit.

Running parallel to Princes Street is Rose Street, at one time something of a 'red light' district, but now lined with small fashion shops, boutiques, jewellers and the like, with plenty of pubs, bars and cafés in between. For more off-beat shops you should visit Stockbridge, a browser's paradise of antiques, boutiques, lighting emporiums and astrology centres, again liberally endowed with cafés and pubs.

To the south of Princes Street, beyond the Gardens, Victoria Street curves down from George IV Bridge to the Grassmarket. Here you will find smart antique and print shops, bookshops, clothes shops, a jokes and tricks shop and, at number 40, what is probably Victoria Street's oldest establishment, Robert Cressers. Opened in 1873 and seemingly unchanged since that time, it stocks brushes and brooms for every eventuality. Go in, and you are stepping back in time. Look around and you are sure to find something you can use, from a birch broom to a dusting brush made with wild boar's hair. They also stock shortbread moulds, porridge spirtles and traditional ridged washing boards.

Cockburn Street linking the High Street with Waverley Bridge, is packed with untidy fashion, record and book shops in a young and lively environment.

Of course, as you travel around Edinburgh, you will not have noticed any shortage of gift and souvenir shops, or stockists of Edinburgh rock, Scottish crafts and traditional merchandise. Indeed, it often seems that the symbolic items – tartan, the pipes, whisky, haggis – are oversold at the novelty end of the market, leaving the casual observer with the impression that there is little else on offer.

The Arts in Edinburgh

The arts scene in Edinburgh is a lively one attributable in no small part to an annual influx of ideas from the festivals. This section of the book lists and describes the theatres, concert halls and cinemas, with telephone numbers for bookings, and gives a selection of museums and galleries to visit.

Scotland's rich and turbulent past has produced a wealth of material to fill the museums and galleries of Edinburgh. From Pictish symbol stones to the work of the Colourist movement, from a Nordic walrus ivory chess set to the writings of Robert Louis Stevenson, the range and variety of exhibits is vast. And, of course, there are treasures and curiosities collected from beyond Scotland's shores – Dutch old master paintings, a stuffed dodo and relics of the Pharoahs can all be found. Museums and galleries recommended in this section highlight a wide range of subjects.

For details of what's on in cinema, theatre, music, art and rock get a copy of The List, a fortnightly publication, or look in the entertainment columns of the daily newspapers. Free information is readily available at the Tourist Information Centres and the Scottish Arts Council Information centre (see below). Your hotel, if you are staying in one, may also be able to help.

General information on the various Edinburgh festivals can be found in the next chapter.

Ticket agencies and information

Scottish Arts Council Information Centre   B3
19 Charlotte Sq. 031–226 6051. An invaluable source of information on exhibitions, festivals and concerts in Edinburgh and throughout Scotland. *Open 09.00–17.30 Mon–Fri (Fri 17.00). Closed Sat & Sun.*

City Art Centre   F4
2 Market St. 031–225 2424 x 6650. In a building designed by Dunn & Findlay 1899–1902 for *The Scotsman* newspaper as a newsprint store, and sympathetically converted to its present use in 1980, the city's permanent fine art collection of about 3000, mainly Scottish works, is beautifully displayed. Dating from the 17thC to the present, works by late 19thC and early 20thC artists are well represented, and contemporary works are continually being added.

There are also temporary exhibitions, a studio, lecture room, shop and a licensed café/restaurant decorated with a mural by William Crosbie RSA. *Open 10.00–18.00 Mon–Sat (Oct–May 17.00), 14.00–17.00 on Suns during Festival. Admission free.*

Edinburgh Entertains   F3
32 Waverley Bridge. 031–225 3732. *Open 10.00–17.00 Mon–Sat, evenings and Sun during the summer.*

Cinemas

Cameo   C7
Home St. 031–228 4141. Popular new releases. *Late shows Fri & Sat.* Bar.

Cannon 1, 2 & 3
Lothian Rd. 031–229 3030. Three cine-mas under one roof showing popular new releases. Bar.

Dominion 1, 2 & 3
Newbattle Terrace. 031–447 2660. A choice of three films. Restaurant and bar. *Closed Sun.*

Edinburgh Filmhouse 1 & 2
88 Lothian Rd. 031–228 2688. A constantly changing array of interesting British, American and Continental films. Restaurant and bar (both *open all day Mon–Sat, bar Sun eve also*) and cinema shop.

Odeon 1, 2 & 3   H7
7 Clerk St. 031–667 7331. Popular new releases. Restaurant and bar.

Concert Halls

The Assembly Rooms   D3
54 George St. 031–225 3614. A rather over grand building designed by John Henderson and opened in 1782. The portico was added by William Burn in 1817. Noted for its season of lunchtime concerts, featuring leading classical musicians and vocalists from Scotland and further afield.

Queen's Hall   H7
87 Clerk St. 031–668 3456. Originally the Hope Park Chapel of Ease, it was very successfully converted to a concert hall in 1979. Hosts a lively and varied programme of concerts, from chamber music to rock, from jazz to opera, and is highly regarded for its atmosphere, accoustics and facilities, which include a bar and licensed restaurant.

Reid Concert Hall   F6
Bistro Sq (sw corner). 031–667 1011 x 4577. Built in 1858 as the Reid School of

Music, and now providing a home for the University Collection of Historic Musical Instruments. Evening concerts of classical and chamber music, free lunchtime recitals.

St Cecilia's Hall G4
Niddry St, Cowgate. 031–667 1011 x 4577. Built in 1763 for the Musical Society of Edinburgh and now opened by the University, who keep the Russell Collection of Harpsichords and Clavichords here. The beautiful oval concert hall was restored in 1968, and provides an ideal setting for performances on these instruments, and for the annual summer Bach festival.

Usher Hall C5
Lothian Rd (at junction with Grindlay St). 031–228 1155. Built in 1914 and paid for by the brewer Andrew Usher, a bust of whom may be seen in the lower crush hall. An imposing domed building of Darney stone, its handsome interior with high vertiginous galleries seats 2780. Concert seasons by the Scottish National Orchestra, the Scottish Chamber Orchestra and other visiting musical ensembles.

Theatres

King's Theatre C7
2 Leven St. 031–229 1201. A traditionally decorated Victorian theatre of 1906 vintage, looking rather as if it should have been built in Glasgow. Recently restored. Regular seasons of the Scottish Opera, pantomime, The Scottish Ballet, popular plays, touring companies, popular singers and solo musicians.

Playhouse Theatre G1
18–22 Greenside Place. 031–557 2590. Opened in 1929 as a dual purpose theatre/cinema seating 3048, and conse-

quently very spacious. Regular seasons by The Scottish Ballet, The Scottish Opera and others. Also rock concerts.

Royal Lyceum Theatre C5
Grindlay St. 031–229 9697. Edinburgh's premier playhouse, built in 1883 and continuously lit by electricity since that date. Fine, richly decorated Victorian interior. Classic plays performed by the resident company, plus the occasional opera. Licensed restaurant and bar.

Traverse Theatre E5
112 West Bow, east end of the Grassmarket. 031–226 2633. Exciting, original and innovative new works by contemporary Scottish and international playwrights. Licensed restaurant and bar.

Museums

The Georgian House B3
7 Charlotte Sq. 031–226 5922. A typical Georgian dwelling on the north side of Charlotte Square, designed by Robert Adam in 1791 and completed following his death in 1792 by Robert Reid. Furnished in 1974–5 as a typical example of the house of a wealthy family during the reign of George III, the stone-flagged entrance hall leads to an inner hall and dining room with a reeded black marble Adam fireplace. To the rear is a bedroom with a fireplace from Tarvit House, Fife. The basement kitchen is particularly fascinating, being equipped with a full range of implements brought from Forglen House. On the first floor are the drawing room and library, the former having an exceptionally fine carved fireplace taken from Number 5, Charlotte Square. Owned by the National Trust for Scotland since 1966 (their headquarters have been at Number 5 since 1949) it gives a valuable insight into the lifestyle of the monied and leisured classes of

18thC Edinburgh. See also The New Town, page 53. National Trust Shop. *Open Easter–Oct 10.00–17.00 Mon–Sat; 14.00–17.00 Sun. Nov 10.00–16.30 Sat; 14.00–16.30 Sun. Closed Dec–Easter. Admission charge.*

Gladstone's Land   E4
477b Lawnmarket (in the Royal Mile). 031–226 5856. When Thomas Gledstanes bought a 16thC building from the Fisher family on 20 December 1617 he initiated a rebuilding programme which survives substantially as we see it today. A curved forestair stands beside an arcaded front enclosing reconstructed shop booths between round pillars which support a typically narrow frontage some five storeys tall and culminating in two equal gables. Presented to the National Trust for Scotland by Miss Helen Harrison in 1934, it was sensitively restored by Sir Frank Mears and Robert Hurd, whose renovations exposed some splendid original work, especially the 17thC wall and ceiling paintings in the first floor front room. Among the fine furniture are some surprising innovations – note the folding bed and wooden 'baby-walker'. Owned by the Gledstanes until well into the 18thC, it remains a superb example of a 17thC town house. *Open Apr–Nov 10.00–17.00 Mon–Sat; 14.00–17.00 Sun; Nov 10.00–16.30 Sat, 14.00–16.30 Sun. Closed Dec–Mar. Admission charge.* Also an art gallery with changing exhibitions of contemporary work. *Open Apr–Oct.*

Huntly House Museum   H4
Canongate. 031–225 2424. Never a great town house as the name implies, but an amalgamation of three houses converted into one in 1570. Bought in 1647 by the Incorporation of Hammermen, who used it as a meeting house, they employed Robert Mylne to enlarge the frontage and convert it into flats. This work was completed in 1671. It takes its

name from George, first Marquess of Huntly, who had lodgings here in 1636. After the building of the New Town, Huntly House degenerated into a slum along with most of the other buildings in Canongate. Its humble beginnings should certainly not discourage a visit however, for the wealth of original fittings, panelling and fireplaces to be seen is quite staggering. The restoration was executed by Frank C. Mears in 1927–32, who • replicated the inscribed Latin panels which gave rise to the building's 19thC nick-name, the speaking house. Rambling through passageways and in rooms on differing levels, the exhibits and period room settings show many examples of the past life of Edinburgh. There are important collections of local silver, glass and pottery, and of particular interest to those exploring the Royal Mile, an excellent miniature reconstruction of how it would have appeared in the 17thC and 18thC. *Open Jun–Sep 10.00–18.00 Mon–Sat; Oct–May 10.00–17.00 Mon–Sat and 14.00–17.30 on Suns during the Festival. Admission free.*

John Knox House Museum   G4
45 High St. 031–556 6961. John Knox was converted from Catholicism in 1542 and became leader of the Reformers in Scotland. His association with this picturesque building is limited to the few months he spent here as a dying man in 1572. Built in the late 15thC from polished freestone, with an outside stairway, it was probably extended in either 1525 or 1544 and remains a prime example of the once common overhanging wooden upper floors with crow-stepped gables. Its original owners were the Arres family, who would have lived above the shops which have always occupied the basement. The interiors, the Oak Room with its original fireplace and 16thC wall painting, and the study, are evocative of life in the

15thC and 16thC. Exterior decorations include a prominent inscription which reads Lufe God abufe al and yi nychtbour as yi self (Love God above all and thy neighbour as thy self), a garlanded coat of arms bearing the initials of James Mossman and Mariotta Arres, and a sundial with a carved relief of Moses. This latter item once incorporated a model pulpit and effigy of John Knox which can now be seen inside. Open Apr–Oct 10.00–17.00 Mon–Sat; Nov–Mar 10.00–16.00 Mon–Sat. Admission charge.

Lady Stair's House   E4
Lady Stair's Close (off the Lawnmarket). 031–225 2424 x 6593. Built in 1622 for Sir William Grey of Pittendrum and purchased in 1719 by Elizabeth, Dowager Countess of Stair. An inscribed lintel above the entrance door bears the date 1622 and the initials of Sir William Grey and his wife. Inside you will find period room settings, and collections of memorabilia relating to the lives and works of Robert Burns, Sir Walter Scott and Robert Louis Stevenson. Open Nov–Mar 10.00–18.00 Mon–Sat; Oct–May 10.00–17.00 Mon–Sat and 14.00–17.30 on Suns during the Festival. Admission free.

Lauriston Castle
2 Cramond Road South. 031–336 2060. The original castle of the Lauristons of that Ilk was burned during the Earl of Hertford's invasion of 1544. The lands were bought circa 1590 by Sir Archibald Napier of Edenbellie and Merchiston, who built a new tower house to the west of the old part (burnt down in 1544) which still stands amidst Jacobean extensions built by William Burn in 1827. Once the home of John Law, financial adviser to Louis XV and the man responsible for introducing paper money to France, there are fine interiors and period and reproduction furniture to be seen, as well as Flemish tapestries

and a superb collection of Derbyshire Blue John ware. The well–tended gardens overlook the Forth. Open Apr–Oct 11.00–13.00, 14.00–17.00 Sat–Thur. Nov–Mar 14.00–16.00 Sat & Sun only. Guided tours only. Admission charge. Gardens open 09.00–dusk Mon–Sun.

Museum of Childhood   G4
42 High St. 031–225 2424. Devoted to the history of childhood, this is a light-hearted, enchanting, colourful, noisy place. Dolls, trains, models, games, mechanical amusements and books crowd the displays. Adults will love it as much as the children. Open Nov–Apr 10.00–18.00 Mon–Sat; Oct–May 10.00–17.00 and 14.00–17.00 on Suns during the Festival. Admission free.

Musical Instrument Collections
Russell Collection of Harpsicords and Clavicords   G4
St Cecilia's Hall, Niddry St, Cowgate. Open 14.00–17.00 Wed & Sat; 10.30–12.30 Mon–Sat during Festival. Admission charge.

Edinburgh University Collection of Historical Musical Instruments F6
Reid Concert Hall, Bristo Sq. A collection of 1000 stringed, woodwind, brass, percussion and folk instruments. Open 15.00–17.00 Wed, 10.00–13.00 Sat; 14.00–17.00 Mon–Fri during the Festival. Admission free. Further information from the Department of Music, Alison House, 12 Nicolson Sq. 031–667 1011 x 4577.

National Library of Scotland   F4
George IV Bridge. 031–226 4531. As you would expect, you will find here an un-rivalled collection of Scottish books and manuscripts. Founded as the Advocates Library in the late 17thC it has held the right of copyright deposit since 1710, and currently contains over four and a half million items, including the Haxton collection of Bibles and much Celtic lan-

The Arts in Edinburgh

guage material.

There is always something stimulating in the Exhibition Room, which hosts displays on a variety of topics, such as The Stuarts in Literature, Legend and the Arts; Scotland and Russia; and Burns in Edinburgh. The extensive Map Collection is kept at 137 Causewayside (031–667 7848), about a mile to the south. *Open 09.30–17.00 Mon–Fri (20.30 during the Festival); 09.30–13.00 Sat; Apr–Sept 14.00–17.00 Suns during the Festival. Closed on public hols. Admission free.*

National Museum of Antiquities   E2
1 Queen St. 031–225 7534. This wholly Scottish archaeological museum was founded by the wonderfully eccentric eleventh Earl of Buchan (1742–1829) those diverse personal collection formed the basis of what we see today. The museum building was designed by R. Rowand Anderson 1885–90 in the style of a Venetian palace; those who harbour doubts about the blank upper walls of red Corsehill sandstone (currently being restored) will see, upon entering, that this building was designed from the inside. The tall gothic entrance hall is outstanding, with its arched galleries decorated with colourful murals by William Hole, illustrating scenes from the defeat of Hako, King of Norway, by Alexander at the Battle of Largs in 1263. Above, stars twinkle from a dark beamed ceiling. The National Portrait Gallery is entered to the left (see below) while to the right are the museum galleries. The diverse and fascinating archaeological collection, dating from pre-history to the present time, includes: the Traprain Silver, a hoard of 4thC Roman silver unearthed at Traprain Law, East Lothian; 13 pieces of a hand carved walrus ivory chess set dating from circa 1150 and found on a beach at Ardroil on Lewis (unfortunately the rest is in the British Museum); a fine

collection of inscribed Pictish stones; and the Monymusk Reliquary, the church-shaped container in which in the 9thC King, Kenneth MacAlpin, took the remains of St Columba from Iona to Dunkeld. There is also an excellent bookshop. *Open 10.00–17.00 Mon–Sat, 14.00–17.00 Sun. Admission free.*

Royal Observatory
Blackford Hill. 031–667 3321. Two miles south of the city centre and superbly sited (see Parks, Gardens and Viewpoints page 68), the Visitor Centre explains the work of the Royal Observatory, illustrated with some of the finest astronomical photographs ever taken. There are also two large telescopes and a collection of antique telescopes to examine. The Observatory moved to this fine Graeco-Italian building from Calton Hill in 1895, when the smoke over 'Old Reekie' became too thick. *Open 10.00–16.00 Mon–Fri; 12.00–17.00 Sat, Sun & public hols. Admission charge.*

Royal Scottish Museum   F5
Chambers St. 031–225 7534. The rather heavy Venetian Renaissance style exterior gives no clue to the extraordinarily fine interior of this building, designed by Captain Francis Fowke and built in three stages between 1866–9. The main hall is a prime example of Victorian skills with cast iron slender pillars (partly replaced with steel in 1955) support galleried aisles with cast iron balustrades, all beneath a glass roof supported on timber arches (now found to have dry-rot and being replaced with steel wrapped in wood, to appear as the original). The whole building is light, elegant and airy giving it an echo of Joseph Paxton's Crystal Palace building for the Great Exhibition held in London in 1851.

Originally called 'The Industrial Museum of Scotland' its location in close proximity to the University, has always been important to its development. Officially opened in 1866 by Prince Alfred (later Duke of Edinburgh), its name was changed to the Royal Scottish Museum in 1904. The University Natural History Collection was transferred to this new building upon its opening, and this provided the basis of what we see today – the skeleton of a blue whale, a stuffed Western Lowland Gorilla and a Gavial, a distinctive Indian crocodile, are among the larger exhibits, together with birds, fish and a Hercules beetle in the entomology department. There are objects from the Middle and Far East, an invertebrate gallery, a fossil gallery and a great favourite, the Hall of Power, full of working models of locomotives, engines and the like, together with the Wylam Dilly, a locomotive which pre-dated Stephenson's more famous Rocket. Occupying the whole of one end of the hall is a giant water-wheel dating from 1862. The museum is a wonderful place for both adults and children. *Open 10.00–17.00 Mon–Sat; 14.00–17.00 Sun. Admission free.*

Scottish Record Office   B3
West Register House, Charlotte Sq. 031–556 6585. A collection of historic documents is on permanent display, and there are facilities for research both here and at the Old Register House in Princes Street (facing North Bridge). Old Register House is the headquarters, built between 1774–1827 to a design by Robert Adam. It is built of stone throughout, to guard against fire and damp. The records date from the 12thC to the present day, and their preservation before Register House was completed was haphazard to say the least. Variously kept in London, Edinburgh Castle and Parliament House in the High Street (where a cat was petitioned for, to keep down the mice) it was not until 1765 that funds were made

available to secure their safe keeping. By the 1960s the 13 miles of shelving were found to be inadequate for the amount of material, so the New West Register House in Charlotte Square was secured. This was built as a new structure inside the shell of St George's Church, built in 1810 to a rather ostentatious design by Robert Reid. The permanent museum displays documents relating to The Declaration of Arbroath, The 'Auld Enemy' (England), The National Covenant, The Treaty of Union, and other topics. *Open 10.00–16.00 Mon–Fri. Closed Sat & Sun. Admission free.*

Galleries

National Gallery of Modern Art
Belford Rd. 031–556 8921. Recently moved from Inverleith House, in the Royal Botanic Gardens, to John Watson's School, a rather country house sort of building designed by William Burns in 1825 for the fatherless children of the well to do, and converted to its present use 1981–4. The collection records the development of painting over the past 100 years, with works by Braque, Picasso, Matisse, Magrite, Miro, Lichtenstein, Ernst, Matthew Smith, Henry Moore and Hockney. There is also a fine collection of recent Scottish works and new acquisitions keep the displays alive. The grounds of the school make a fine backdrop for the larger modern sculpture. Naturalists should look out for the mistletoe, very rare in Scotland, growing in the large lime tree just inside the entrance gate. It is thought to have been seeded by birds feeding on plants introduced onto some hawthorns in the old Dean Cemetery by William Paxton. Very pleasant licensed restaurant in the basement, open same hours as gallery. *Open 10.00–17.00 Mon–Sat; 14.00–17.00 Sun (18.00 during the Festival). Admission free.*

National Gallery of Scotland   E4
The Mound. 031–556 8921. This rather severe Greek temple to the south of the Royal Academy houses a collection of 1000 paintings, with works by virtually all the Old Masters. The old Royal Institution began the collection in the 1830s, and it was given great impetus in 1946 with the loan of the Duke of Sutherland's collection, which included works by Raphael, Rembrandt and Titian. Its recent audacious purchasing policy has resulted in further major works being acquired.

The scale of the gallery, not over large, naturally limits the pictures on display to those of particular importance, thus preventing the visitor from being totally overwhelmed by the sheer number of works. Renovation of the gallery, which will inevitably cause some disruption, should be completed during 1988. *Open 10.00–17.00 Mon–Sat; 14.00–17.00 Sun, (18.00 during the Festival). Admission free.*

Royal Scottish Academy   E3
The Mound. 031–225 6671. Another of Playfair's Greek temples, this one was built in 1826 and enlarged in 1836. Inside, the work of academicians and invited artists, with an annual summer exhibition held from the end of April to early July. *Open 10.00–19.00 Mon–Sat; 14.00–17.00 Sun. Admission charge.*

Scottish National Portrait Gallery   E2
1 Queen St. 031–556 8921. Sharing the building with the National Museum of Antiquities, this collection dates from 1882 and illustrates all the major figures in Scottish history from the mid 16thC onwards, including Mary Queen of Scots and Robert Burns. The Scottish Photography Archive is also here, and there are temporary exhibitions. *Open 10.00–17.00 Mon–Sat, 14.00–17.00 Sun. Admission free.*

Talbot Rice Gallery   G5
University of Edinburgh, Old College, South Bridge. 031–667 1011 x 4308. One part of this gallery houses the university's permanent collection, including some notable 17thC Dutch paintings and a number of 16thC and 17thC bronzes, the other is given over to temporary exhibitions, such as contemporary Scottish artists or touring exhibitions from abroad. *Open 10.00–17.00 Mon–Sat. Closed Sun. Admission free.*

The Edinburgh Festival

For the last three weeks of August each year, Edinburgh plays host to what is probably the greatest cultural extravaganza on earth, a truly international festival of the arts, embracing music, theatre, dance, film, books, painting and photography. It is supported by a boisterous fringe festival which spills over onto the streets, giving this usually restrained city a colourful, carnival atmosphere. Filled to overflowing with some of the world's most talented performers, audiences come in droves from all over the world, making Edinburgh the place to be. The atmosphere also infects the local residents during August; they support their festival to the hilt.

The Edinburgh Military Tattoo, although not officially part of The Festival, takes place at the same time, and its matchless setting against the floodlit backdrop of the Castle adds pageantry and occasion to the calendar of events. The sounds of the massed pipes and drums echo over the city centre, and the noise of cannon fire can be heard three miles away in Portobello.

Film buffs, jazz fans and book worms can all indulge at their own festivals within The Festival, and there are many events specifically for children. It has happened every year now for over four decades, growing each year to the present 300 plus performances, with an incredible 1000 Fringe events. There is now even a fringe to the Fringe. It was the idea of impressario Rudolf Bing and H. Harvey Wood, the then Director of the British Council in Scotland. It all came to fruition in 1947, in a gloriously warm August against the background of rationing and post-war austerity. The opening concert was given by the Orchestre des Concerts Colonne of Paris and critics acclaimed the new festival a success.

Each year's programme is unique, and may have a central theme – Scottish Enlightenment in 1986 for example, or the Soviet emphasis of 1987. The following brief descriptions will give you an idea of the structure of the Festival.

Music

The Usher Hall is the main concert venue, and a Gala Opening Concert is held there, followed throughout the three weeks by chamber music, more orchestral concerts, choral works, piano recitals and the occasional modern musical. The beautiful Queen's Hall sees a series of concerts by smaller ensembles – individual performers, duos, quartets and so on, and there are usually one or two concerts in St Giles' and St Mary's cathedrals. The spectacular Glenlivet Fireworks Concert is staged mid-way through the Festival at the Ross Bandstand in Princes Street Gardens, when the Scottish Chamber Orchestra perform to the backdrop of a spectacular pyrotechnic display.

Opera and Music Theatre

Standard and new works are performed by visiting companies plus the Scottish Opera Orchestra at the King's Theatre and the Leith Theatre.

Dance

The Playhouse Theatre and King's Theatre stage spectacular ballet and folk dance productions by visiting companies. Matinee performances are given with reduced prices for adults accompanied by children.

International Theatre

From Shakespeare to puppetry and from comedy to folk-mythology, the best of theatre from all over the globe graces the stages of the King's Theatre, the Royal Lyceum St Bride's Centre, Church Hill and Leith Theatres.

British Theatre

Hard to predict what you may find – historical drama or poetry, contemporary comedy or jazz dance, folk tales or readings in the Scottish dialect, there is sure to be something that appeals. Venues include the Assembly Hall, the Church Hill Theatre, the Playhouse Theatre, St Cecilia's Hall and the St Bride's Centre.

Exhibitions

The major galleries and museums – National Gallery of Scotland, the Royal Scottish Academy, the Modern Art Gallery and the reputable Richard Demarco Gallery – all stage special exhibitions for the Festival.

Children

A special programme highlighting events thought to be of particular interest to children is widely available during the three weeks. There are often greatly reduced ticket prices for matinee performances. Some of the best entertainment for children, however, is free – every afternoon by the side of the Royal Scottish Academy (on the corner of The Mound and Princes Street) a number of jugglers, fire eaters, magicians, acrobats, musicians and clowns perform for everyone's delight.

The Fringe

Nearly as old as The Festival itself, it is usual for about 450 companies to give over 1000 performances at around 140 different venues in the space of three weeks. The present Fringe still adopts the same principle as the eight companies who performed outside the official programme in 1947 – each group or individual simply invites itself. No artistic selection is made. The Edinburgh Festival Fringe programme now extends to 96 pages of comedy, revue, children's shows, music, opera and exhibitions and rather belies its unofficial status.

Exciting, adventurous, ridiculous, speculative and outrageous, the Fringe exudes creative energy that spills out onto the streets. It is often superb, but sometimes appalling. Some shows, by challenging orthodox ideas and succeeding, go on to join the establishment – *Beyond the Fringe* in 1960 provided a launching pad for Jonathan Miller, Alan Bennett, Peter Cook and Dudley Moore and broke new ground for British humour. Other shows fail to run their allotted span. How do you sort the good from the not so good? Read the reviews, *The Scotsman* is well informed about what's going on, or listen to the talk in the pubs but never be afraid to take a chance! Whatever you choose, try not to miss the Festival Calvalcade, an afternoon procession along Princes Street on the opening Sunday, or Fringe Sunday, at the end of the first week, a feast of free entertainment in Holyrood Park from 13.00 onwards. Samples of many of the shows plus circus acts, jugglers, magicians, face painting and kite flying. Great for a picnic.

The Fringe Fringe Society

It had to happen, and in 1987 it did. Companies that miss the official Fringe deadline for bookings are accommodated here at The Edge Theatre in Drummond Street.

International Film Festival

From modest beginnings in 1947, when it concentrated mainly on documentary films, the Film Festival, running concurrently with the main festival, now has a world-wide reputation for its wide range of subject matter – from experimental video to new Holywood feature films. Film directors often appear personally to explain their new work. Many have their world or British première at the Festival. It is all based around The Filmhouse, in Lothian Road.

International Jazz Festival

For five days during The Festival a choice selection of top bands and performers play at such places as the Queen's Hall, The Amphitheatre, Platform 1, The Cotton Club, with a gala night at the Usher Hall. Altogether over 350 performances in around 20 venues.

Book Festival

By no means a long-established event – indeed 1987 saw only the third biennial Book Festival, staged in the superb setting of Charlotte Square – but an exciting and interesting new dimension to The Festival.

Thousands of British and international books to see and buy, visiting authors, computer demonstrations, children's specialities, lunchtime readings, cabaret, food tastings and so on – a very full literary programme.

The Edinburgh Military Tattoo

An event officially separate from The Festival but now an inseparable part of the whole occasion – a spectacular, exciting, noisy and sometimes moving display each evening (except Suns), ending with a fireworks display on the late Saturday performances. It first began in 1950 and still thrills the crowds with mock battles, highland dancing, gymnastics, pageantry, horse-riding and of course the music of the massed pipe bands. All floodlit at dusk on the Castle Esplanade against the fairytale edifice of the Castle itself. It ends with one spotlight on a lone piper on the battlements, playing a farewell lament.

Festival Facts

During the three weeks of The Festival about three-quarters-of-a-million visitors come to Edinburgh, with the result that there is a great demand for accommodation, tables in restaurants and tickets for the main Festival events. If you like to be sure of what you are doing, clearly you must book ahead. Do not let this dissuade you, however, from coming to The Festival at short notice – experience suggests that accommodation can be found, although choice will be restricted, and there are so many performers covering such a wide range of tastes, that there's sure to be plenty to enjoy. Just to come at Festival time, soak up the atmosphere and enjoy the free street performances can be a reward in itself. The following names, addresses and phone numbers, hints and tips should enable you to sort things out. Ticket prices are, generally speaking, very reasonable. Information, in the form of free leaflets and handouts, abounds – and creates a tidal wave of litter.

Edinburgh International Festival
Edinburgh Festival Society F4
21 Market St, Edinburgh EH1 1BW. 031–226 4001. Programme and ticket order form usually available during April, and you can then book by post immediately. Personal counter bookings begin mid-May. During July you can book by telephone using your credit card – ring 031–225 5756. This number does get very busy, however, and you may have difficulty getting a reply. An alternative is to book through First Call on (London) 01–240 7200, which is a 100-line, 24-hour seven days a week service, but they charge a booking fee.

Tickets can also be obtained from:
Ticket Centre on Waverley Bridge F3
Otherwise book through 5000 UK travel agents who have access to Edwards & Edwards on PRESTEL 22021187. These are for best seats only, and incur a booking fee. Half price tickets are available on the day from a booth at the bottom of The Mound. It is open 13.00–17.00, and tickets are sold on a first-come first-served basis, restricted to two per customer.

The Festival Information Centre E4
In the car park of The National Gallery on The Mound will supply up-to-the-minute information on ticket availability for all performances. Open 10.00–18.00 Mon–Sun during the Festival. Disabled people should request the leaflet Festival Venues – A Guide for Disabled People, which gives all the necessary information, plus details of Artlink, the free escort service.

The Festival Club F5
9–15 Chambers St. Box office and information: 031–220 1112. Daily theatrical performances, live music (especially as a major Jazz Festival venue), exhibitions, two restaurants, snack bar, licensed bars and souvenir shop. Open 10.00–02.00 every day during The Festival.

Edinburgh Festival Fringe F4
170 High St, Edinburgh EH1 1QS. 031–226 5257 or 5259. (The new Fringe Office, when open, will be in the close beside the old office). Programme and ticket order form usually available early July, and you can then book by post immediately. Personal counter bookings are taken every day from the end of July, as are telephone credit card bookings (Access and Visa), 031–226 5138.

The Fringe Club F6
Teviot Row, Bristo Sq (end of George IV Bridge). 031–667 2091. Late night cabaret and entertainment during The Festival. Membership (available here or at The Fringe Office) is necessary. Food, drink,

snooker and showers available. *Open 10.00–03.00 Mon–Sun.*

The Fringe Fringe Society   G5
Drummond St. 031–557 5229. Head-quarters and box office. Very informal.

The Edinburgh Military Tattoo
Tattoo Office   F4
22 Market St. 031–225 1188. Postal book-ings are accepted from 1 *January* at this address. Personal counter sales begin at the Ticket Centre, Waverley Bridge, from *early July.*

The Edinburgh Book Festival   D2
25a South West Thistle Street Lane. 031–225 1915. All tickets are available from 1 July for Theatre events detailed in the programme by post from this address, or in person at the Fair, from the Edin-burgh Bookshop, 57 George St (*Mon–Sat*) and The Fringe Office. Telephone credit card sales (Access or Visa) on 031–220 1259. Tickets for the Book Festival only are bought at the door, on the day.

Edinburgh International Jazz
Festival Office   J3
116 Canongate. 031–557 1642. Pro-gramme and booking information.

Edinburgh International Film
Festival Filmhouse   B5
88 Lothian Rd. 031–228 2688. Programme and booking information usually available during June.

Edinburgh's Other Festivals

Edinburgh International Folk Festival
For 10 days during *April*, the city hosts a series of Ceilidhs and concerts, work-shops and courses, presented by home-grown and foreign artists. A special feature of the first weekend is the Edinburgh Harp Festival. For infor-mation ring 087–530 298.

Spring Fling
A community-based fortnight of events and activities, ranging from try-it-yourself sports, art exhibitions, theatre, music, parties, galas, discos, dancing, poetry, cycling, writing and competi-tions. Over 100 events, most of them free. Details from the Arts Outreach Team 031–225 2424 x 6623 or 6625, or the Recreation Marketing Unit 031–557 2480. A programme detailing everything that goes on is produced well in ad-vance.

Sports & Games

Having twice played host to the Commonwealth Games, it naturally follows that Edinburgh is well-endowed with sports facilities. In this chapter information on the city's main sports centres and national sports is accompanied by a description of that most Scottish of occasions, the Highland Games. For the spectator Highland Games offer everything – the excitement of a close run race, trials of strength, demonstrations of skill, Scottish dancing and the pipes, all in a jolly, convivial atmosphere.

For the keen golfer, Scotland is a major world venue. The game originated here – but whether in Edinburgh or St Andrews is an argument that will continue for years. What is beyond question is that those who love golf will find the choice of courses in and around the city second to none. We have listed those where you will be able to play a round or two at short notice, without needing a personal introduction, plus details of the historic courses of St Andrews and the beautiful links at North Berwick.

It is, of course, the Highlands which offer some of the world's finest fishing, but if you're not travelling north there is sport to be had around the capital in rivers, lochs and reservoirs.

If you want to watch a game of rugby at Murrayfield, or a football match, book an hour's squash, or go for a swim then read on.

Sports Centres

Craiglockhart Sports Centre

177 Colinton Rd. 031–443 0101. 2½ miles south west of the city centre. Originally the Craiglockhart Club operated by the East of Scotland Lawn Tennis and Sports Club, it was converted into a multipurpose sports centre in 1976 although it still remains one of Scotland's major racquet sports complexes, with 4 badminton courts, 6 squash courts and 18 tennis courts (6 grass, 12 all-weather). This is where the Scottish grass court tennis championships take place. Canoeing and sailboarding are taught on the lake, and aerobics, archery, fencing, fitness training, table tennis and yoga are all offered. A crèche operates during women only sessions, there is a senior citizens activity club, under 10's sessions and summer sports schools. Many of the facilities are open to non-members, but only members can book in advance. *Open 09.00–23.00 Mon–Sun (22.30 Sat & Sun). Admission charge.*

Hillard Ski Slope

Biggar Rd. 031–445 4433. Artificial ski slope with two main runs of different standards, both 400m, plus a tow slope of 260m and a nursery slope of 50m. All slopes are watered every half hour. Full equipment hire. Tuition every evening (except Thur), Wed afternoon, Sat & Sun morning. Cafeteria with bar and restaurant facilities. *Open Sep–Apr 09.30–22.00 Mon–Sun; May–Aug 09.30–21.00 Mon–Fri; 09.30–17.00 Sat & Sun. Admission charge.*

Jack Kane Sports Centre

208 Niddrie Mains Rd. 031–669 0404. 4 miles south east of city centre. Named after former Lord Provost, Dr Jack Kane, this large complex offers the following: 2 five-a-side football halls, 8 badminton courts, hockey pitch, 2 outdoor tennis courts, 11 football pitches, rugby pitch, American football pitch, an outdoor all-weather training area, fitness training room, combat and keep fit area and BMX and cycle speedway tracks. A crèche operates during women's keep fit sessions, and there are special facilities for the under 10's, including Marvin, the giant inflatable monkey. The facilities are open to non-members, but only members can book in advance. *Open 09.00–22.00 Mon–Sun. Admission charge.*

Meadowbank Sports Centre and Stadium

139 London Rd. 031–661 5351. Half a mile east of city centre. A 25-acre indoor and outdoor sports complex built for the 1970 Commonwealth Games and refurbished for the 1986 Games. It is a major venue for national and international athletics events, which results in the facilities often not being available for periods during the summer. As well as the excellent athletics stadium with facilities for track and field, there is also archery, badminton, fencing, gymnastics, health and fitness training, judo, squash, rock climbing, table tennis, trampolining, weight training and wrestling. Cyclists will relish the superb velodrome. There is a crèche facility for women only sessions, senior citizens sessions, and a special 'soft play area' for children, particularly for those with special needs (group bookings only for this). Many of the facilities are available to non-members, but only members can book in advance. *Open 09.00–21.30 Mon–Sun. Admission charge.*

Murrayfield Ice Rink

Riversdale Crescent. 031–337 6933. Regular public skating sessions, for which you can hire skates. Tuition available and ice hockey most Sunday evenings

Sep–Apr. Refreshments. *Open 14.30–16.30 Mon–Sun. Admission charge.*

Royal Commonwealth Pool
Dalkeith Rd. 031–667 7211. Although this large complex is now beginning to show its age, it is still excellent for serious swimmers and learners, with the added blessing of an ozone water purification system which avoids sore eyes. Fifty metre main pool, twenty metre learners pool and a deep diving pool with boards at 5m, 7.5m and 10m, and springboards at 1m and 4m. You can book excellent tuition, there is a multi-gym, a sauna and martial arts facilities. Water temperature is often quite chilly by present day standards. *Open 09.00–21.00 Mon–Fri, 10.00–16.00 Sat & Sun. Admission charge.*

Saughton Sports Complex
Stevenson Drive. 031–444 0422. 2 miles west of city centre. A new complex with floodlit all-weather facilities, which include synthetic running track, tennis courts and football pitches plus full size and five-a-side grass football pitches. Book one week in advance for football (031–661 5351 for the grass pitches) and tennis, but just turn up for the running track. *Open 09.00–20.30 Mon–Sun. Admission charge.*

Fishing

With an abundance of clean rivers, lochs and reservoirs supporting rich populations of native brown trout, it is not surprising that fishing is a popular local pastime. And with the added attraction of sea trout and salmon in the Rivers Esk and Almond, excellent sport may be had without venturing as far as the Highlands. Full details of where to fish, and where to obtain permits may be found in *A Guide to Fresh Water Fishing in the*

Lothian Region, obtainable free from the Department of Planning, Lothian Regional Council, 12 St Giles St, Edinburgh EH1 1PT. 031–239 9292 x 2559.

Football

Played on Saturday afternoons from September to April, Scottish league football tends to lose some of its finest players to the wealthier English clubs, but many top international players can be seen in the Scottish Premier League. The game is very much alive and well here. The two Edinburgh clubs are:
Heart of Midlothian (Hearts)
Tynecastle Park, Gorgie Road. 031–337 6132. Founded in 1874, they last took honours in 1979–80, when they were First Division champions.
Hibernian (Hibs)
Easter Road Stadium, Albion Road. 031–661 2159. Formed in 1875, they were First Division champions 1980–1.

Golf

Although St Andrews in Fife claims to be the world centre of golf, Edinburgh can justly vie for this title, since it was in 1744 that the Honourable Company of Edinburgh Golfers recorded in their minute book the first written rules of the game, prepared for a competition to be held at Leith. Of course, golf had been played for hundreds of years prior to that date, seemingly without the need for written rules. James VI of Scotland, when he became James I of England in 1603, took the game with him to London, giving rise to another claim that the Royal Blackheath Club, formed in 1608, is the oldest club in the world. This may be true in the formal sense, yet it is known that regular, if informal, gatherings of golfers were a common

Highland Games

An integral part of the Scottish summer, these gatherings provide a colourful spectacle, with the kilt and the pipes very much in evidence, and the opportunity to see some unique trials of strength, such as tossing the caber and the 'weight for height' competition.

They have existed in more or less their present form for just 200 years, although the clansman's need for fitness and strength, and a natural competitive urge, has probably seen such trials of strength over a much longer period. Indeed King Malcolm III (1056–1093) is thought to have founded the first hill race (a feature of the present larger Highland Games) on the Braes o'Mar on Royal Deeside when he needed to find the swiftest messenger. He is also said to have created the intricate sword dance to celebrate his killing of Macbeth at Lumphanan in 1050. This is, of course, just speculation, but the events themselves still reflect the traditions of the clans – a tough outdoor life and gatherings to petition their leaders. The villagers of Ceres in Fife claim that their games, held annually on the last Saturday of June, are the oldest, dating from the return of the village bowmen from the Battle of Bannockburn in 1314.

Tossing the caber is perhaps the most widely known competition, a unique exercise requiring a sound technique, great strength and balance. The caber is 5.5m long and weighs 68 kilos and, when thrown must describe a 180° arc before landing vertically. Style is everything.

In the weight-for-height event each competitor stands beneath a bar, over which he has to hurl a 25 kilo agricultural weight. The bar is gradually raised, and may reach a height of 4.5m. Less experienced participants swing the weight upwards and run, lest the weight should fall on their head. Old hands stand immobile as the weight thuds into the ground behind them. Hurling the hammer can prove hazardous for the spectators when a throw goes awry – and competitors are known to have been knocked unconscious by the implement.

Perhaps one of the most ancient events is simply the lifting of heavy stones – 'clach cuid fir' or manhood stones. Famous examples are the Stones of Dee at the Bridge of Potarch on Deeside and those outside the churchyard at Balquihidder. Hill running, tug o'war, high and long-jumping, hurdling and other athletic events usually complete the sporting itinerary, which will be liberally interspersed with piping displays and dances. Best known is the Highland Fling, said to have been derived from the mating antics of the stag.

A part of Scotland's tradition not to be missed, you can see Highland Games not too far from Edinburgh at:
Strathmiglo, Fife. *Early Jun.*
Ceres, Fife. *Late Jun.*
Cupar, Fife. *Early Jul.*
Burntisland, Fife. *Mid Jul.*
Airth, Falkirk. *Late Jul.*
Dunfermline, Fife. *Early Aug.*
Pestonpans, East Lothian. *Late Aug* and of course all over Scotland from *May–Sep,* with the most famous being at Braemar in *early Sep* and arguably the largest at Cowal, near Dunoon, in *late Aug.* A free leaflet giving complete details is produced by the Scottish Tourist Board, and local Tourist Information Centres will also provide information.

occurrence in Scotland much earlier than this. Where else other than in Scotland would you find a sign ordering 'No Golf' positioned by a tiny square of rough grass in a housing estate?

An astonishing 28 courses lie within Edinburgh's boundaries and there are over 80 within 20 miles of the city centre. One of the first, although now abbreviated to a short pitch and putt course, was Bruntsfield Links, on common land overlooked by Ye Olde Golf Tavern, which itself dates from 1456. There are moorland courses set amidst dramatic hill country, bracing coastal courses among the dunes, and parkland courses with tree lined fairways and carefully planted shrubs, yet one of the city's most notable golfing contests did not take place on a course at all, but in Parliament Square in 1798. William Smellie, instigator of the *Encyclopaedia Brittanica* and publisher of Burns' poems, and a Mr Scales of Leith tried to settle a dispute by hitting golf balls over the top of the crown of St Giles' Cathedral, some 49m high. Each man successfully cleared the obstacle with six balls, which came to rest in Advocate's Close, off the High Street. Further down the Royal Mile, in Canongate, is Golfer's Land, commemorating a house built by John Pattersone with the proceeds of a golfing wager, when he successfully partnered the Duke of York (later James II) in a contest at Leith Links. His original plaque, which bears the motto 'Far and Sure', can still be seen. The following courses and clubs are those which place few, if any, restrictions upon visitors, and, with a couple of notable exceptions, are fairly close to the city centre.

Braid Hills Golf Courses
Braid Hills Rd. 031–447 6666. Off the A702, 2½ miles south of city centre. Municipal. 2 courses: 18 holes, par 70,

5731 yards. 18 holes, par 65, 4832 yards.

Carrick Knowe Golf Course
Balgreen Rd. 031–337 1096. A8, 2 miles west of city centre. Near Murrayfield. Municipal. 18 holes, par 71, 6299 yards.

Duddingston Golf Club
Duddingston Road West. 031–661 7688. A1, 3 miles south of city centre. 18 holes, par 72, 6647 yards. Visitors welcome *Tue & Thur only.*

Kingsknowe Golf Club
326 Lanark Rd. 031–441 1145. A70, 3 miles south west of city centre. 18 holes, par 68–69, 5979 yards. Visitors restricted at weekends.

Liberton Golf Club
Kingston Grange, 297 Gilmerton Rd. 031–664 1056. A68, 2½ miles south east of city centre. 18 holes, par 67, 5299 yards.

North Berwick Golf Club
West Links, North Berwick. 062–026 66. About 22 miles north east of city centre. Follow the A198. Included here since it is considered by many to be the finest links course in Scotland. Its situation, overlooking Fidra, with the Bass Rock and Isle of May in the distance, is superb. 18 holes, par 70, 6298 yards.

Portobello Golf Course
Stanley St, Portobello. 031–669 4361. A1, 3 miles east of city centre. Municipal. 9 holes, par 32, 2405 yards.

St Andrews
Fife. 033–475 757. 55 miles from Edinburgh city centre. It must be every golfer's ambition to play on the historic Old Course at St Andrews, the world centre for golf. All the four courses here are open to visitors, but demand is brisk so booking is advisable. Firm bookings for

the Old Course can be made up to nine months in advance, or you can take your chances with the daily ballot. Visitors must have a handicap certificate or a letter of introduction from their club. Old Course: 18 holes, par 72, 6566 yards. New Course: 18 holes, par 71, 6604 yards. Eden Course: 18 holes, par 69, 5971 yards. Jubilee Course: 18 holes, par 70, 6284 yards.

Silverknowes Golf Course

Silverknowes Parkway. 031–336 3843. 4 miles north west of city centre, near Cramond. Municipal. 18 holes, par 71, 6214 yards.

Turnhouse Golf Club

154 Turnhouse Rd, Corstorphine. 031–339 1014. Off the A8 near Edinburgh Airport, 5 miles west of city centre. 18 holes, par 69, 6171 yards.

Torphin Hill Golf Club

Torphin Rd, Colinton. 031–441 1100. 3 miles south west of city centre. 18 holes, par 67, 5025 yards.

Rugby

With a fanatical following in the Lowlands and Borders, the spiritual home of Scottish Rugby Football is:
Murrayfield Stadium, Roseburn St. 031–337 2346 (Scottish Rugby Union). International matches have been played here since 1925, and two of the home international series are played here some time between *Jan–Mar* each year. Other special games, including those with touring sides, are staged throughout the season, which lasts from *Sep–Apr*. Club matches are played each Saturday on the back pitches.

149

Edinburgh Directory

Some hints and information to make your visit run smoothly, plus where to go for help if things do, unfortunately, go wrong. The great majority of Edinburgh folk are polite, courteous and friendly, so never be afraid to ask for help or advice should you need it.

Accommodation

Tourist Information and Accommodation Bureau, Waverley Market, 3 Princes St. 031–557 2727.

Tourist Information and Accommodation Desk, Edinburgh Airport. 031–333 2167. The city has a reputation for providing good accommodation and polite and courteous service throughout the price range – from smart hotel to modest bed & breakfast in a suburban house. The accommodation bureaux give an excellent service, but if you want to arrange your own guest house or B & B, the areas to head for are Broughton, Liberton, Morningside, Newington and Murrayfield.

Hotels in Central Edinburgh

It is compulsory for hotels to display their prices. Visitors should make sure exactly what is included in the price, ie breakfast, VAT, service etc. We have given price guidelines for each hotel: £ = £25 and under; ££ = £25–£45; £££ = £45–£65; £££+ = £65 and over.

Many hotels have facilities for conferences, banquets, receptions etc but in each entry we refer to this as conference capacity.

Key: Conference capacity = Conf cap; Swimming pool = S pool; Parking = P; Leisure Centre; Central heating = CH; Credit cards: Access = A, American Express = Ax, Diners = D, Visa = V.

Ailsa Craig   J1
Royal Terrace. 031–556 6055. Beautiful Georgian terrace near major attractions. 14 rooms all with attached shower, some with bath. CH. TV. Conf cap 30. A. £.

The Albany   F1
39–43 Albany St. 031–556 0397. In a quiet terrace just a few minutes walk from town centre. 21 rooms all with bath. CH. TV. Conf cap 30. A.Ax.D.V. £££.

Cairn   H1
10–18 Windsor St. 031–556 1120. Well reputed hotel in nice setting. 52 rooms all with shower, some with bath. CH. TV. A.Ax.D.V. ££.

Caledonian   B4
Princes St. 031–225 2433. Grand old hotel right in the centre of town. 238 rooms with bath. CH. TV. Conf cap 300. P. A.Ax.D.V. £££+.

Carlton Highland   F4
North Bridge. 031–556 7277. Large well reputed hotel close to Waverley station. 207 with bath. CH. TV. S pool. Leisure centre. Conf cap 200. A.Ax.D.V. £££.

Edward   D1
58 Great King St. 031–556 1154. Small but popular hotel in the New Town. 15 rooms. 7 with bath. CH. A. £.

The George E2
19 George St. 031–225 1251. Well known hotel right in the heart of the New Town. 195 rooms all with bath. CH. TV. Conf cap 50. A.Ax.D.V. **£££**.

Hotel de France F3
8–10 St Andrews St. 031–556 8774. Adjoining Princes St and close to all major attractions. 30 rooms with bath. CH. TV. Conf cap 30. A.Ax.D.V. **£££**.

Howard Hotel D1
Great King St. 031–557 3500. Elegant central hotel. 25 rooms all with bath. CH. TV. Conf cap 50. P. A.Ax.D.V. **££**.

King James (Thistle) F2
St James Centre. 031–556 0111. Convenient to return to after a day exploring the city. 147 rooms all with bath. CH. TV. Conf cap 80. A.Ax.D.V. **£££**.

Ladbroke Dragonara
Belford Rd. 031–332 2545. Superb hotel just west of Princes Street. Special feature is the granary bar created from the original 19thC mill. 146 rooms all with bath. CH. TV. Conf cap 100. P. A. Ax. D. V. **£££**.

Loch Ewe J1
21 Royal Terrace. 031–556 6749. In lovely Georgian terrace within walking distance of town centre. 32 rooms all with shower, some with bath. CH. TV. A. Ax. D. V. **£**.

Lindon E1
Nelson St. 031–556 4344. Small and friendly with bar for non residents. 20 rooms nearly all with bath. CH. TV. Conf cap 20. A.Ax.D.V. **£**.

Mount Royal E3
53 Princes St. 031–225 7161. Overlooking the gardens and the Castle. 159 rooms nearly all with bath. CH. TV. Conf cap 70. A.Ax.D.V. **££**.

Old Waverley E3
43 Princes St. 031–556 4648. Occupies one of the finest positions on Princes Street. 66 rooms, all with bath. CH. TV. Conf cap 50. A.Ax.D.V. **££**.

Park J1
33 Royal Terrace. 031–556 1156. Ideally situated in lovely Georgian crescent. 28 rooms, nearly all with bath. CH. TV. A. **£**.

Roxburghe B3
Charlotte Sq. 031–225 3921. Situated in the beautiful West End. 76 rooms all with bath. CH. TV. Conf cap 50. A.Ax.D.V. **£££**.

Royal British F3
Princes St. 031–556 4901. Traditional hotel now being newly refurbished. 77 rooms nearly all with bath. CH. TV. Conf cap 120. Overnight parking facility. A.Ax.D.V. **££**.

Royal Terrace H1
17–20 Royal Terrace. 031–556 5879. Old hotel now being refurbished. 70 rooms all with bath. CH. TV. Leisure Centre. Conf cap 30. A.V. **£££**.

Sheraton B5
Lothian Rd. 031–229 9131. Newest luxury hotel in the city. 263 rooms all with bath. CH. TV. S pool. Leisure centre. Conf cap 480 (largest in the city). P. A.Ax.D.V. **£££+**.

Stakis Grosvenor
Grosvenor St. 031–226 6001. Spacious and well kept hotel. 136 rooms all with bath. CH. TV. Conf cap 80. A.Ax.D.V. **£££**.

Transport

Air

Edinburgh Airport
031–333 1000. Six miles west of the city centre with good road access and a useful airlink bus service from Waverley Bridge. A first rate internal service with regular shuttle flights to London Heathrow, Gatwick and Manchester and international services operate from here. Duty free shop, gift shop, restaurant, buffet and bars. Facilities for the disabled.

Buses

Lothian Regional Transport   E2
14 Queen St. Bus enquiries 031–226 5087. Edinburgh is well served with buses. A time table may be obtained from the Ticket Centre, Waverley Bridge, and general details of routes are displayed on the front of each bus and bus numbers are displayed at each stop. Exact change is needed for the ticket machines which are situated by the driver at the front of the bus. Or you can buy a pass, which allows you to go anywhere as often as you like in the period it is valid for. Car drivers should note that many of the main routes into the city are marked with bus lanes on the left hand side, and should leave these clear for buses during the morning and evening rush hours.

Coaches

Coach Station   E2
St Andrews Sq. 031–556 8464. Coaches to all major destinations in England and Scotland. National Express and Scottish City Link both operate from here. Phone bookings not accepted.

Trains

Waverley Station   G3
031–556 2451. The very best way to arrive in Edinburgh is by train, since the main station, Waverley, nestles beneath the Castle, amidst the gardens and is overlooked by the Scott monument and Princes Street. Get off at Haymarket Station for the west of Edinburgh. High speed Inter-City 125 trains run frequently to London, with a journey time of about five hours. There are also services to Glasgow, Stirling, Dundee, Inverness, with connecting services to Stranraer, Oban, Mallaig, Kyle of Lochalsh, Wick and Thurso.

There is an information desk at Waverley Station, or you can ring the above number for details of trains (calls are stacked, so hang on until you get an answer).

Cars

Car hire
A car can easily be hired by anyone who has held a full driving licence for at least one year, is between the ages of 25 and 65 and has a 'clean' driving licence, or minor offences only. Expect difficulties, restrictions or extra expense if you fall outside any of these requirements. Ring around several companies for prices, bearing in mind what use you are to make of the car, ie. short period/high mileage, longer period/low mileage, big car/small car. Rates will be presented differently by each company, and comparisons can sometimes be difficult. All the major companies – Avis, Budget, Godfrey Davis, Europcar, Hertz – have offices in the city, and there are many, many other local firms. They are all listed in the *Yellow Pages* telephone directory, which can be found at main post offices.

Driving

Visitors can drive on a valid foreign licence for a maximum period of 12 months. In Scotland, as in the rest of the UK, you drive on the left. Road signs are similar to those used in the rest of Europe. Speed limits are as indicated or, if not indicated, 70mph on motorways and dual carriageways, and 60mph on other roads and 30mph in built up areas. A single yellow line at the kerbside indicates no daytime parking (see signs close by), a double yellow line indicates no parking at any time. Zig-zags near pedestrian crossings also indicate no parking at any time. Drivers and front seat passengers must wear seat belts by law. Dipped headlights must be used in poor daytime visibility. Drink-driving laws are rigorously enforced, so soft drinks if you are driving.

Although most petrol in the UK is leaded, unleaded petrol is becoming more widely available. Two star petrol is low octane, four star is high octane.

Traveline: A recorded message giving information on roadworks and possible delays throughout Scotland. 031–246 8021.

Useful Information

Emergency

If you are involved in an emergency, and require the services of the Police, Fire Brigade, Ambulance Service or Coastguard, **dial 999**. The call is free from any telephone.

The procedure is – ask for the service you require – when connected give them the number shown on the telephone you are using, the address where help is needed and any other useful information.

Chemists

Boots   B4
48 Shandwick Place. 031–225 6757. *Open*

08.45–21.00 Mon–Sat, 11.00–16.30 Sun.

Consulates

Australia   E3
80 Hanover St. 031–226 6271.
Belgium
89 Constitution St. 031–554 3333.
Denmark
50 East Fettes Avenue. 031–552 7101.
France   A3
11 Randolph Crescent. 031–225 7954.
Germany (Federal Republic)
16 Eglinton Crescent. 031–337 2323.
Italy   A4
2 Melville Crescent. 031–226 3631.
Netherlands   E2
8–12 George St. 031–225 8494.
Norway   C3
86 George St. 031–226 5701.
Spain
4 Chester St. 031–226 2991.
Sweden   H4
6 Johns Place. 031–554 6631.
Switzerland
6 Moston Terrace. 031–667 1011 x 6366.
USA   J2
3 Regent Terrace. 031–556 8315.

Dental treatment

A full list of dental surgeons will be found in the *Yellow Pages* telephone directory. For emergency dental treatment:
Dental Hospital and School   F5
31 Chambers St. 031–225 9511. *Open* 09.00–10.15, 14.00–15.15 Mon–Fri.

Disabled People

Artlink: an escort and transport service is available for anyone with a disability to visit arts events in Edinburgh. Ring 031–557 3490.

Doctors

Visitors to the UK can usually arrange free treatment at a local Health Centre. Lists of these can be obtained from police stations or the telephone directory, and hotels usually have this information.

If you are staying longer than three months you can register with the National Health Service, which will entitle you to free treatment. Careful checks are made to ensure that visitors do not exploit this situation by entering the country with a serious illness in the hope of receiving free treatment. Enquiries to:

Lothian Health Board
Primary Care Department, 14 Drumsheugh Gardens. 031–225 1341.

Prescriptions for medicines should be taken to a chemist/pharmacy to be prepared. A standard charge is payable.

Drinking

Alcoholic drinks are sold for consumption in pubs, licensed restaurants (with food) and hotel bars. Standard pub opening times are 11.00–14.30, 17.00–23.00 Mon–Sat; 12.30–14.30, 18.30–23.00 Sun. But many have regular extension licences which allow them to stay open all day, and later at night. Residents in licensed hotels can buy a drink at any time. Young people under the age of 18 are not allowed to consume alcoholic drinks on licensed premises – some will allow them in, accompanied by adults, for soft drinks, some will not. Some pubs have special 'family rooms'. If in doubt, enquire.

Bottles of beers, wines and spirits can be purchased from wine shops or off-licences (liquor stores) as well as licensed grocers and supermarkets.

Hospital Casualty Departments

In case of a serious accident or sudden life-threatening illness, dial 999 and ask for an ambulance. In other cases of injury or acute illness, make your own way to the nearest hospital Casualty Department. All are open 24 hours. Those most central are:

Leith Hospital
Mill Lane. 031–554 4433.
Royal Infirmary of Edinburgh
1 Lauriston Place. 031–229 2477.
Western General Hospital
Crewe Rd. 031–332 2525.

Libraries

Edinburgh Central Library   E5
George IV Bridge. 031–225 5584. Open 09.30–20.30 Mon–Fri; 09.30–13.00 Sat. Closed Sun.
National Library   F4
George IV Bridge. 031–226 4531. Open 09.30–20.30 Mon–Fri; 09.30–13.00 Sat. Closed Sun.

Lost property

Enquire at the nearest Police Station or:
Police Lost Property Office
Fettes Avenue. 031–311 3131.
Railway Lost Property   F3
Waverley Station. 031–556 2477. Open 08.30–17.00 (16.30 Fri), 08.00–12.00 Sat. Closed Sun.
Bus Lost Property   E2
14 Queen St. 031–554 4494. Open 09.00–13.00, 14.15–17.00 Mon–Fri.

Money

Visitors may bring in as much currency and travellers' cheques as they wish. Notes are issued by the three Scottish banks – Bank of Scotland, Clydesdale, Royal Bank of Scotland – to the value of £50, £20, £10, £5 and £1. Coins are issued to the value of £1, 50p, 20p, 10p, 5p, 2p and 1p; there are 100 pennies (p) to one pound. All Scottish and English notes are interchangeable.

Banks: City banks are usually open 09.30–15.30 Mon–Fri and a few open on Sat morning. Closed Sun and public hols. There are many cash dispensing machines outside major banks, which can be used, with the appropriate card, outside these hours.

Bureau de Change
Tourist Information Centre   G3

Edinburgh Directory

Waverley Market, Princes St. *Open 08.15–20.00 Mon–Sat, 11.00–21.00 Sun.*
Main Post Office   G3
2–4 Waterloo Place. 031–550 8232. *Open 09.00–17.30 Mon–Fri, 09.30–12.30 Sat. Closed Sun.*
Many of the large hotels also offer exchange facilities.

Post Offices
These are usually open from 09.00–17.30 Mon–Fri, 09.30–12.30 Sat. Closed Sun. Smaller post offices will close for lunch, 13.00–14.00.
Edinburgh Main Post Office
2–4 Waterloo Place. 031–550 8232.

Public Holidays
These do not coincide with public holidays in the rest of the UK, and can vary from city to city in Scotland. Banks and commercial offices will close, but shops will often remain open. Dates vary from year to year, but when public holidays do occur, they are usually on a Monday.

Shopping
Shops are usually open from 09.00–18.00 Mon–Sat, with only smaller suburban shops observing an early closing day, which is usually Wednesday. Many large stores remain open until 20.00 on a Thursday, and many tourist shops are open on Sunday.

Overseas visitors, who buy goods for export, can often reclaim the 15% VAT which is levied. Enquire at time of purchase, and expect to have to fill in some forms.

Telephones
Full operating instructions are given in each telephone directory. Virtually all calls are now dialled direct, indeed 98% of overseas calls are made this way. However, your usual point of contact, should you need to enquire, is the operator – dial 100. For directory enquiries,

dial 192. Calls are less expensive during the afternoon, and cheapest from 18.00–08.00, with other special rates applying to overseas calls.

The minimum coin needed for payphones is 10p. For calls within the Edinburgh area, omit '031' at the beginning of the number. Cards for card phones are obtainable at newsagents and post offices.

Tickets
For tickets for the Edinburgh Festival, see page 142. Otherwise contact:
The Ticket Centre   F4
Waverley Bridge. 031–225 8616.

Tourist Information
Tourist Information Centre   F3
Waverley Market, 3 Princes St. 031–557 2727. An excellent centre giving all sorts of information regarding what's on in the city, and details of sights. Free literature, bookshop, accommodation bureau and bureau de change.

The small local Tourist Information Centres spread throughout Scotland are invaluable sources of local information – always call in when you are travelling.

Weather
There are many unfair myths circulating about Scotland's weather. Whilst there are places on the western side where the rainfall is high, Edinburgh's annual total is the same as that of southern England, as is the average July temperature. In common with most of the eastern side of the UK, there is plenty of sunshine. If there is a problem, it is the east wind, which during the winter comes from north eastern Europe funnelling through Edinburgh's wide streets. It can chill you to the bone.
Weatherline: 031–246 8091 for a recorded forecast for the Edinburgh and Lothian region.

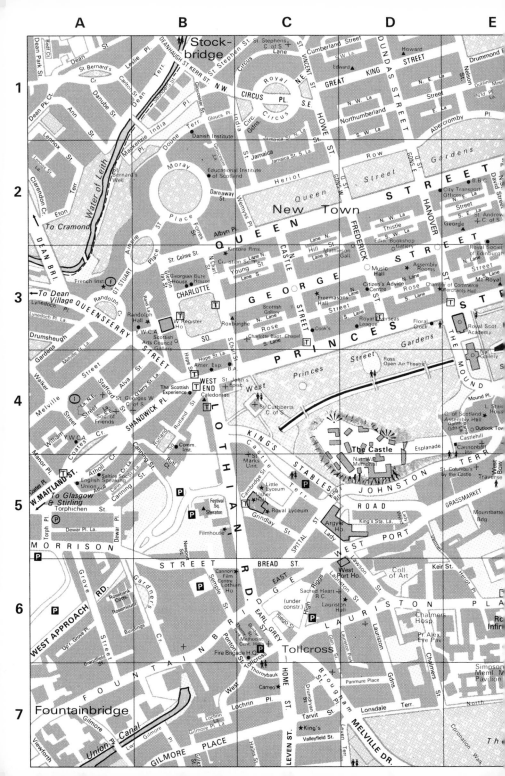

Index

Index

Index